I DON'T SUPPOSE YOU WOULD REMEMBER ME BUT I USED TO FOLLOW YOU BACK IN SIXTY-THREE

JEREMY R. RICHEY
220 TUPELO TRAIL 1607
FRANKFORT, KY 40601
VOLUME 1/JANUARY, 2019/FIRST PRINTING
NOSTALGIAKINKY.COM

THIS VOLUME IS DEDICATED TO THE MEMORY OF KATHY KERR

HAVE YOU SEEN ME?

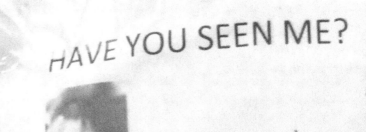

White cat with black fur on head, b
nose, probably wearing a red safet
bell. May respond to "Mikey" or "
from Clay Street. Any info, call: 39

THIS VOLUME OF SOLEDAD CONTAINS

INTERVIEWS WITH CRAIG BELL,
JOHN D. MORTON AND STOYA

FICTION BY LES BOHEM AND ROBERT MONELL

ESSAYS BY HEATHER DRAIN, TARA HANKS
AND JEREMY R. RICHEY

PHOTO ESSAYS BY
IAN PRESTON CINNAMON, JOHN LEVY
AND JEREMY R. RICHEY

POETRY BY EMILY CLARE BRYANT

A BOOK EXCERPT BY MARCELLINE BLOCK

CONCEPT, EDITING, PUBLISHING,
PHOTOGRAPHY (UNLESS OTHERWISE NOTED)
AND CUT-UP CREATIONS
BY JEREMY R. RICHEY

Cover Quote from *Double Feature* by Terence Stamp.
Front, Side and Back Page Quotes by Pete Townshend.

ANGER, DENIAL, BARGAINING, DEPRESSION, ACCEPTANCE.

TWENTIETH CENTURY-FOX & COLUMBIA PICTURES PRESENT IN A

ROY SCHEIDER BOB FOSSE FILM ALL THAT JAZZ

ALSO STARRING
JESSICA LANGE ANN REINKING LELAND PALMER SPECIAL GUEST APPEARANCES **CLIFF GORMAN & BEN VEREEN**

DIRECTOR OF PHOTOGRAPHY **GIUSEPPE ROTUNNO** EDITOR **ALAN HEIM** PRODUCTION DESIGNER **PHILIP ROSENBERG** FANTASY DESIGNER **TONY WALTON** MUSIC SUPERVISOR & CONDUCTOR **RALPH BURNS**

EXECUTIVE PRODUCER **DANIEL MELNICK** PRODUCED BY **ROBERT ALAN AURTHUR** ASSOCIATE PRODUCERS **KENNETH UTT & WOLFGANG GLATTES**

COLOR BY TECHNICOLOR® NOW IN PAPERBACK FROM JOVE

DIRECTED BY **BOB FOSSE** WRITTEN BY **ROBERT ALAN AURTHUR** AND **BOB FOSSE**

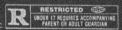

"This is something that I dream about:
to live films, to arrive at the point at which one
can live for films, can think
cinematographically, eat
cinematographically, sleep
cinematographically, as a poet, a painter,
lives, eats, sleeps painting."

-Bernardo Bertolucci, 1941-2018-

Farewell maestro and thank you....

THE

SEEKER

BY

JEREMY

RICHEY

TELL ME ABOUT JENNY!

Terence Stamp, un homme qui est traqué par... le futur.

Sylvana (Jeanne Moreau) a proposé à Terence une expérience étrange.

Cycle Francs-tireurs

HU-MAN

UN FILM DE JÉRÔME LAPERROUSAZ (1975)

SCÉNARIO DE
JÉRÔME
ET GUILLAUME
LAPERROUSAZ
FRANCIS
GUILBERT
ET ANDRÉ RUELLAN

IMAGES DE
JIMMY GLASBERG

MUSIQUE DE
DAVID HOROWITZ,
JEAN GUILLOU ET
PATRICK VIAN

DURÉE : 1 H 30

--- NOTE CRITIQUE ---

SCIENCE-FICTION. Magnifique sujet, prétexte, pour Jérôme Laperrousaz, à une débauche d'images somptueuses, un maelstrom de bruit et de fureur, où la musique tient un rôle inattendu. ⑦

Terence Stamp	**Terence Stamp**	Franck	**Franck Schwake**
Sylvana	**Jeanne Moreau**	Gabriella	**Gabriella Rystedt**
Viviane	**Agnès Stevenin**	L'homme-oiseau	**Yannis Thomas**
Frédérick	**Frédérick Van Pallandt**	Le technicien de régie	**Bob Traynor**

LE SUJET

De nos jours. Un acteur célèbre, bouleversé par la mort de sa femme, accepte de participer à une expérience scientifique dangereuse : un saut dans le futur.

SI VOUS AVEZ MANQUÉ LE DÉBUT

Dans son château de la région bordelaise, vit, retiré du monde, l'acteur Terence Stamp. Depuis la mort de sa femme, Viviane, trois ans plus tôt, il refuse toute proposition et n'accepte que la présence, épisodique, de Gabriella, une adolescente, amoureuse de lui en secret. Mais voici que débarque chez lui Sylvana, une actrice

Terence et Gabriella (Gabriella Rystedt) qui l'aime en secret.

qui fut sa maîtresse avant son mariage avec Viviane. Elle vient lui proposer, pour le compte de l'Institut des recherches temporelles, d'être le premier voyageur à

évoluer à travers le temps. Avant de prendre sa décision, Terence demande à rencontrer les dirigeants de l'Institut, dont le directeur, Frédérick, se montre particulièrement convaincant. L'expérience doit se dérouler en deux temps : face à des caméras de télévision, le comédien devra risquer sa vie, et c'est l'énergie émotionnelle produite par les téléspectateurs qui permettra de passer à la seconde phase, le saut dans le futur. Avec obligation, sous peine de mort, de revenir au point de départ...

Cote Télé 7 Jours :	Office Catholique :
	pour adultes

It's the summer of 1974 and Terence Stamp has found himself at the hottest spot on earth. He's drenched in sweat, dehydrated and standing near a rumbling active volcano with scorched bubbling lava surrounding him on every side. He's alone save for a small film crew in the distance attempting to stay away from the harms way that Stamp has so firmly placed himself in.

Ethiopia's Danakil Depression has been called both a 'gateway to hell' and an 'alien world'. Sitting at over 400 feet under sea level, it is one of the most isolated, dangerous and strangest spots on earth and it marks the final location for Jérôme Laperrousaz's haunting and mesmerizing science fiction oddity *Hu-Man* (1975).

All but lost for nearly forty years, *Hu-Man* recently reappeared without warning via a number of torrent sites and finally YouTube. A mind-melting mixture of documentary and fantasy, *Hu-Man* is quite unlike any film ever made and it makes for a disturbing and hypnotic viewing experience.

The volcanic land and acidic lakes of the Danakil Depression might serve as the most memorable location in *Hu-Man* but the majority of the film was shot throughout France in the summer of 1974. Focusing on a depressed and disillusioned actor (Stamp) who is given the opportunity to star in a 'reality television show' that will give him the chance to either go back in time or into the future, the at times confused plotting of *Hu-Man* is the least compelling thing about it as it is ultimately a spectacular visual exercise and nothing short of an audacious cinematic exorcism.

Jérôme Laperrousaz was just in his mid twenties when he wrote and directed *Hu-Man* in 1974. The young filmmaker had two documentaries under his belt by the time he began preparing his otherworldly narrative debut. His previous film, *Continental Circus* (1972), had focused on the world of motorcycle racing while his first feature, *Amougies (Music Power - European Music Revolution)* (1970) documented a music festival that featured Captain Beefheart, Frank Zappa, Yes and Pink Floyd! Music would remain a chief concern with *Hu-Man* as it features a wild soundtrack by Animals and War vocalist Eric Burdon among others.

Working closely with cinematographer Jimmy Glasberg and editor Noun Serra (both of whom had previously worked on *Continental Circus*), Laperrousaz surrounded himself with all relative cinematic newcomers behind the scenes and in front of the camera, save for Stamp and co-star Jeanne Moreau. In fact, for many, the film was a one-off as a number of the players both on screen and off wouldn't work on another film again. *Hu-Man* doesn't feel amateurish in any way though. This is an accomplished and powerful work guided by a sharp cinematic eye and a triumphant lead performance from an actor who was very much lost in the woods in 1974.

Terence Stamp owned the sixties. Possessing one of the most beautiful faces in film history, not to mention one of the finest screen actors ever seen, Stamp it seemed could do no wrong early on. A pivotal player in the swinging London scene of the sixties, Stamp was immortalized by Ray Davies in The Kinks "Waterloo Sunset", was seen regularly with some of the world's most beautiful women, had an Oscar nomination by his mid-twenties and alternated easily between box-office hits and art-house favorites and then Jean Shrimpton happened.

The stunning Shrimpton was just as unstoppable as Stamp was in the sixties. Among the earliest examples of a true 'supermodel', Shrimpton was the primary muse to famed photographer David Bailey throughout the early to mid sixties (a personal and professional relationship that would help inspire *Blow-Up*) and remains perhaps the key fashion and style icon of the period.

Stamp was preparing for one of the great roles of his career in *The Collector* (1965) when he first met Jean Shrimpton. Stamp described the January 1964 meeting, at a wedding he was attending, in his masterful book *Double Feature*, "I caught a glimpse of her as the sunlight, broken up by the coloured glass in the chancel windows fell upon her face, still angel-innocent...she was my dream girl." Stamp fell madly in love with Shrimpton and they became one of the premiere celebrity couples of the era. They were photographed constantly together and, for a period, seemed like the coolest and most ideal couple imaginable. Stamp adored her to the point of obsession and his, at times, unnerving adoration of her and their time together was still palatable when he wrote about it more than two decades later in *Double Feature*. For Stamp, Shrimpton seemed to represent more than just perhaps the great love of his life. As Fitzgerald once wrote, "youth is a dream, a form of chemical madness."

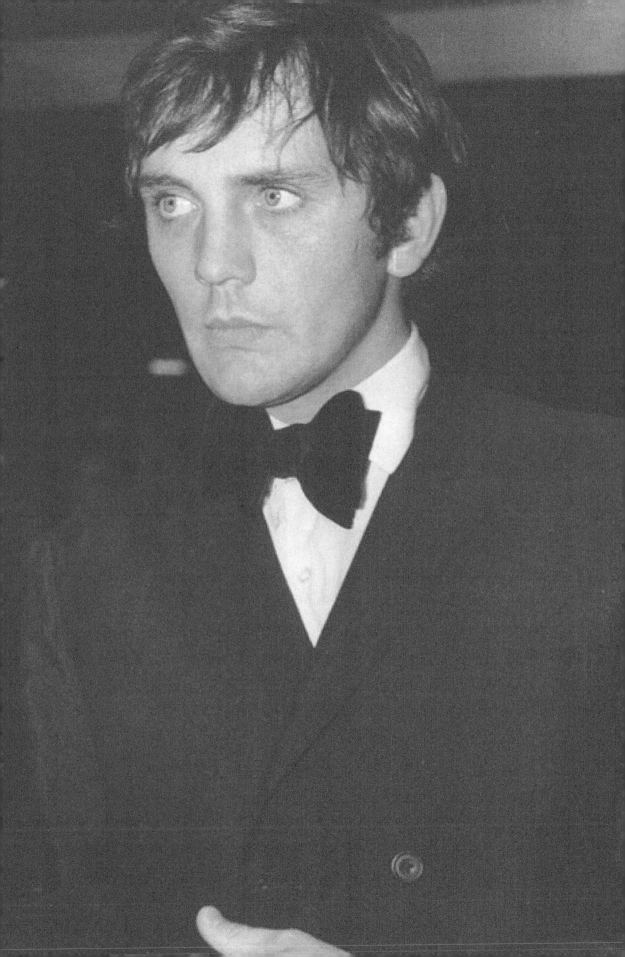

As the only real promise youth offers us is that it will fade, the relationship between Stamp and Shrimpton began to sour as the sixties turned increasingly darker. Their relationship flamed out as Stamp's career began to falter and he entered into a hazy period of sad affairs, hallucinogenics and missed opportunities...all of which coincided with a failed suicide attempt that he describes in great detail in *Double Feature*. All of this would help fuel Stamp's greatest performance, the same year as his suicide attempt, as the haunted title character in Fellini's masterpiece *Toby Dammit* in 1968. This was quickly followed by another jaw-dropping role in Pasolini's stunning *Teorema* (also 1968). For a brief moment it appeared that Stamp would carry on but then, just as quickly as he had appeared in the early sixties, he all but vanished.

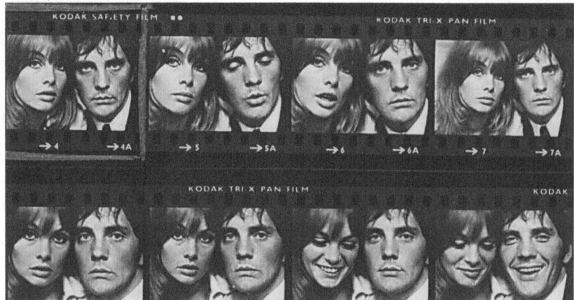

Falling under the spell of the Indian philosopher Jiddu Krishnamurti, Stamp left the crumbling swinging London of the sixties, and the film industry, behind and went on spiritual journey that would eventually find him traveling in India. He would describe this period of exit and eventual rebirth as, "the era over almost before it started. Our era. The gold of the section fading fast...the very own dark start that leads me on, that takes me to far-flung dusty corners."

When Stamp reappeared in 1970 he seemed very much a changed man. No longer the perfect looking beauty who it seemed had youth eternally in his corner, the new Stamp possessed a certain world-weariness and sadness about him.

In the years after *Toby Dammit* and *Teorema* leading up to *Hu-Man*, Stamp would appear in just two films, the strange *The Mind of Mr. Soames* (1970) and the little-seen *A Season In Hell* (1971), a film that would find him playing the doomed poet Arthur Rimbaud. Neither made any kind of real impact and, by the time he made *Hu-Man*, the Stamp of the sixties seemed like a distant memory...a near made up figure of a mythic time very had much passed.

The specter of the sixties and Shrimpton haunts every frame of *Hu-Man* and Stamp's bruised and devastating performance. At times, the film almost feels like a form of psychotherapy and Stamp's work is as naked and brilliant as his great acting hero Marlon Brando's turn in *Last Tango in Paris* a few years earlier. Laperrousaz's work of course doesn't come near the heights reached by Bertolucci's great work of art but it never attempts to...instead its main goal seems to be rescuing one of our greatest actors from a self imposed personal and professional exile. Stamp would tell Mark Cousins more than 15 years after making *Hu-Man* that the film was "basically trying to kill me. It was taking me to some of the most dangerous places on earth". He even recalled telling a cameraman during one of the volcano shots, "'Don't stop shooting me, unless I am really in danger' and when they finished the take a piece of lava had burned itself right through my trousers." It's hard to imagine another actor going quite so far emotionally and physically in a work that, as Stamp admitted to Cousins, would never really have an audience.

A tale of two Stamps. Terence as seen above in 1968, just before his vanishing act and, to the right during the 1974 reemergence just before he filmed Hu-Man.

Hu-Man played to just a select few upon a near non-release in 1975 before it made its way to a few scattered film festival screenings throughout the rest of the decade. Rumors have surfaced about a dispute between the producers and Haroun Tazieff, the famed vulcanologist who helped with some of the films most treacherous shots. Reactions from those who did get to see it during its failed initial attempts at a run were, not surprisingly, mixed as *Hu-Man* is, at its core, a supremely uncompromising vision that was never going to appeal to an audience at large. In many ways its instantaneous slide into cinematic obscurity was oddly fitting...tragic as *Hu-Man* is a truly extraordinary film...but fitting.

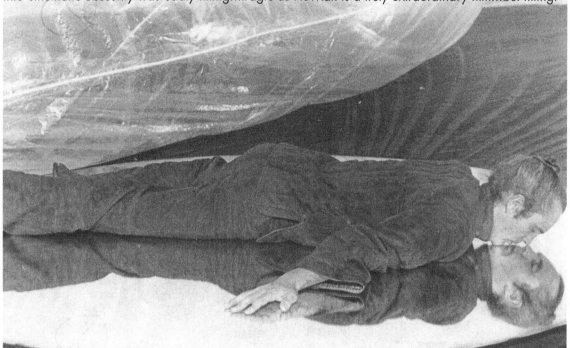

After languishing for decades as an absolutely lost work, the BFI restored 25 minutes of *Hu-Man* for a 2013 tribute to Stamp. These fragments of Laperrousaz's profoundly personal project finally briefly brought the film back into public view. Film journalist Mark Gordon Palmer, who witnessed the screening, called it, on his blog *Seat At The Back*, "among the best 25 minutes of footage I've seen at the cinema" and that it represented "my favourite performance from Stamp, even on just this evidence alone." The timing seemed right for a full restoration, and a Change.org petition was even set up by Scottish filmmaker Robert Gemmell, but more than five years after that BFI screening it still hasn't happened. Thankfully, in the fall of 2015, a fully uncut print of *Hu-Man* was uploaded to the now shuttered French torrent site t411. Reportedly taken from an early beta or VHS recording of the sole 1977 French television broadcast, this upload finally allowed fans the opportunity to see Terence Stamp's most mythic role, albeit via a full-framed washed out print that does the film few favors. This version was quickly shared amongst many of the most popular torrent sites until finally a fan subtitled version was uploaded to YouTube, for all to see, on Christmas Eve in 2017.

Hu-Man seemed to rattle the legendary Stamp out of his artistic slumber and, shortly after making the film, he began to work with renewed regularity and within a few years he made an astonishing commercial comeback as the crazed General Zod in Richard Donner's worldwide blockbuster *Superman* (1978). The eighties and nineties would see Stamp becoming a literary phenomena via his superb multi-volume memoir and his work in films such as *The Hit* (1984) and *The Limey* (1999) are the equal to any of his, or any of his peers, greatest performances.

The now eighty year old Terence Stamp remains one of the most respected actors in the world and each year adds more and more films to his resume, although he has admitted he wishes he could have retired after *The Limey*, as he considered that role to be the true culmination to his career in front of the camera.

Whether of not *Hu-Man* ever gets the full restoration it deserves remains a mystery, but the fact that we can now all easily view one of the most dazzling and unique films of cinema's greatest decade is something that should very much be celebrated by all of those who value art that is both unapologetic and uncompromising.

Portraits by Terry O'Neill and David Bailey. Film stills from *Hu-Man, Toby Dammit* and *Blue*.

GALA WORLD PREMIERE
DECEMBER 12TH

FOX THEATRE/ATLANTA
(4000 seats)

for the benefit of
**THE BURT REYNOLDS
GEORGIA PEACE OFFICERS
SCHOLARSHIP FUND**

SOLD OUT!!

OPENS NATIONALLY
ON DECEMBER 18TH
1200 Theatres

**"STYLISH-
LOOKING,
HARD-NOSED
THRILLER.**
Reynolds succeeds
remarkably well in
capturing the shady
world in which Sharky
is forced to exist.
The cast has been
unusually well chosen,
which is the mark
of a good director."
—Kathleen Carroll,
New York Daily News

**"MURDEROUS
SUSPENSE.**
It's rough, tough,
mean and dirty.
A picture of
uncommon
excitement."
—Archer Winsten,
New York Post

"A roller coaster ride from one breathtaking sequence to another."
—Bob Thomas, Associated Press

BURT
REYNOLDS
SHARKY'S
MACHINE

**"FAST AND
EXCITING.**
Burt Reynolds is as
valuable behind the
camera as he is in
front of it."
—Janet Maslin,
The New York Times

**"A ROUSINGLY
FULL-BODIED
ENTERTAINMENT.**
Reynolds seems to
rise to new levels
of expression as
an actor.
One of the most
stylistically
authoritative
and
refreshingly
un-self-conscious
entertainments
of the
holiday season."
—Andrew Sarris,
The Village Voice

BURT REYNOLDS in

A Deliverance Production film "SHARKY'S MACHINE" starring VITTORIO GASSMAN · BRIAN KEITH · CHARLES DURNING · EARL HOLLIMAN · BERNIE CASEY · HENRY SILVA
DARRYL HICKMAN · RICHARD LIBERTINI and RACHEL WARD as "DOMINOE" Music Supervision by SNUFF GARRETT Director of Photography WILLIAM A. FRAKER, A.S.C.
Screenplay by GERALD DI PEGO Based upon the novel by WILLIAM DIEHL Produced by HANK MOONJEAN Directed by BURT REYNOLDS

Gene Hackman is
Harry Moseby
in an Arthur Penn
Production of a
Warner Brothers Film

Night Moves

"Where were you when
Kennedy got shot?"

"Which one?"

WARNER
COMMUNICATIONS

...ISOLATION

A PHOTO-ESSAY BY
IAN
PRESTON
CINNAMON

Ian Preston Cinnamon was born on March 21, 1975 in Sacramento, California, USA.
He is primarily a director and photographer,
but has been credited as an actor and camera assistant as well.
Ian is also the creative mind behind the acclaimed aTelecine,
one of the most extraordinary musical acts of the past decade.

Follow Ian and aTelecine at atelecine.bandcamp.com and twitter.com/atelecine.

Teenage Blues Triptych:
The Pom Pom Girls, Blue Summer
&
The Last American Virgin

by Heather Drain

Growing up is hard. Not as hard as losing a limb while in the middle of guerrilla warfare, hosting an especially ugly intervention, or wrangling a rogue Osmond, mind you, but still. It can be some rough stuff. Adolescence is painful and being a teenager? Forget it. Youth is something that you get often punished for. The prison-like approach of public schools coupled with the pressure of being forced to know exactly what you should be grabbing for your adult life are just some of the unfair things you weather. Hormones and trying to establish a sense of true self makes it all a fairly spicy combination.

Being a teenager is also that prime time to rebel, explore and build up those emotional scabs that will heal into some good, thick scars to learn from in your adult years. Nailing all of the above in an honest way that stands out from the wild, woolly pack of modern teen films reigns supreme in its trickiness. Many of the teen films I grew up were often alien to my own existence. Films like *Return of the Living Dead* (1985) or

Liquid Sky (1982) were more relatable than any John Hughes flick or even worse, Cameron Crowe's faking-the-funk script for the apogee-of-overrated, *Fast Times at Ridgmont High* (1982). (Seriously, if you subtract Sean Penn, Phoebe Cates' nudity and Judge Reinhold in general, it would fall flatter than a souffle served to you by King Frat himself.) Both *Return of the Living Dead* and *Liquid Sky* dealt with themes of alienation more honestly than a lot of teen-based films of the 1970's and 80's.

But not all of them.

In fact, there are three very notable films that are intertwined by their naturalism, hormonal verve, and the growing pains that come with the slings and arrows of transcending from child to adult. These films are also united by being some of the most overlooked and undervalued of the sub-genre, with only two of the three netting a Blu Ray release by the year 2018. Poorly received by critics, which is often the fate of a film that only gives you some of what you want but will most definitely give you everything you deserve.

1976's *The Pom Pom Girls* is the light before the long, sad-eyed though glorious Teenage Blues Triptych tunnel. It's also a fascinating film, combining an air of naturalism, likable but realistically flawed characters, and a slight dash of teenage whimsy to help keep the proceedings breezy. Written and directed by Joseph Ruben, who would go on to helm the Edsel of teen-sex-comedies, *Gorp* (1980), as well as the taut horror film, *The Stepfather* (1987), *The Pom Pom Girls* may center around the titular girls of pep, but it is so much more.

The opening shot begins with a fiery football player effigy being dropped off the school roof, thanks to the rival team from Hardin High. It's a stark and ugly way to open a film entitled *The Pom Pom Girls*. In other words, it is a veritable valentine to its audience. The flaming ghastly ends pretty quickly as the film cuts to the girls rounded up beachside in bikinis, practicing their cheers while footage is inter-cut with the football team practicing right before the school year begins. These scenes paint an instant picture of two important characters in this film. The football coach, played by prolific character actor James Gammon, is a slight-head case with his air-and-brain-ways filled with power trip assholery.

The other character is Johnnie, who may be one of the most affable high school football players in film history, largely thanks to a blazing performance by Robert Carradine. An underrated actor, Carradine's natural charisma, and innate talent shine like an active volcano here. His Johnnie is alternately cocky, vulnerable, impulsive, and so lovably gangly. Our introduction to him is seeing him practice with the Coach yelling "Move it! Move it!" while Johnnie is running and muttering under his breath, "fuck you...fuck you..." Johnnie's that best friend that you love fiercely even though he is what psychologists refer to as a "Teflon screw-up."

Joining Johnnie in day-to-day quests for fun, burgers, love, and occasional trim is his bestie and fellow teammate, Jesse (Michael Mullins). On paper, Jesse is your 1970's prototype of a high school Lothario, right down to this pimped out van with a bed in the back. In actuality, he still is, but Mullins' performance coupled with some of the character touches from Ruben makes Jesse as cocky as he is insecure and petulant. In short, you know, like an actual teenager.

The girls, while all really beautiful (hey, this is still a 1970's drive-in film called *The Pom Pom Girls*), they are also mercifully Becky free. What is a Becky? A Becky is a muy irritating daddy's girl whose insecurities are often masked by vices such as condescension, shallowness, and plebeian tastes. Just ask Sir Mix-a-Lot. Of the girls, the two that capture Johnnie and Jesse's attention and hearts are Sally (Lisa Reeves) and Laurie (Jennifer Ashley).

Sally is a classic 1970's era, Californian girl. She's all flaxen-haired, blue eyes, and sporting a perma-stoned grin. All that's missing is a back pocket full of Tuinols and an orange-red skateboard. Her boyfriend Dwayne (1970's exploitation-film stalwart Bill Adler), is none too keen on Johnnie's blatant flirtation with his girl. Sally's initial mild-irritation to eventual dumping Dwayne for Johnnie throws some big-sized rock salt into the wound. Over the course of the film, the two fist-fight in a dirty alley, fist-fight on the bleachers during a pep rally, have an aborted food-fight in the cafeteria and end up competing in a game of Suicide Chicken during the film's climax. Typically, a character like Dwayne would be either a predatory Zabka-like bully or a beefy-alpha-male-lunk. Dwayne, though? Neither one. He's considerably less impulsive than Johnnie and probably a bit saner. Also, the guy knows how to work on cars and again, Bill "Van Nuys Blvd" Adler.

Jesse chases Laurie off and on, despite being sidetracked by the occasional fling with another Pom Pom Girl, Sue Ann, played by future wife of the late jazz singer Al Jarreau, Susan Player. Strong willed, with wild dark hair and discerning taste in suitors, Laurie is instantly put off by Jesse's bad reputation, referring to him as the "class stud" with a healthy portion of disgust. Even when some of the other girls, like Sue Ann and Roxanne (the ethereal and criminally underutilized here, Cheryl "Rainbeaux" Smith), get all dreamy-eyed just being near the Van Master, Laurie is having none of Jesse or Johnnie's nonsense.

Well for a spell at least.

So many teen films were written from the point-of-view of what the writers wished high school life had been for them. Pranks and sexual hi-jinks can become so over the top that they border on gloriously brain dead surrealism. The Pom Pom Girls does not quite go there, but it does flirt with it. The highlight of which being the firetruck scene. Targeting their number one rivals and west-coast-pigskin-mooks over at Hardin High, the boys along with ¾ of the girls, visit the neighboring town, waltz into a fire station and effortlessly steal a fire truck, all with the aim of spraying down their rivals during football practice. Not only do they achieve this but also manage to evade the law in the form of Hardin Policeman, generic brand Roscoe P. Coltrane. It's a funny sequence though it is a bit of a reach that none of the kids suffer any consequences for breaking more than a few laws in this adventure. Then again, it's a cute-as-hell reach, so it all works out.

The charisma and natural-acting chops of the main cast, especially Carradine, anchor the film and do right by a refreshing though semi-flawed script. Helping cement this little film as a teenage-gem-in-the rough though is the camerawork and cinematography, all in the more than capable hands of Stephen M. Katz. Katz has lensed everything from Jack Hill's 1975 classic, *Switchblade Sisters* to Bill Condon's 1998 film, *Gods & Monsters*. More than capable hands is an easy descriptor with a director of photography like Katz.

The Pom Pom Girls is a film that goes beyond its exploitation-style clothing. Granted, it doesn't go wickedly beyond, but it has enough respect for the audience to have characters who make both good and bad decisions and even grow-up a little bit in the process in ways that feel more authentic and less hackneyed. It's also proof that Robert Carradine should have been a much bigger star. He's absolute magic here.

From dirt bike roads and grand theft auto to an all American coming-of-age road trip story, Chuck Vincent's 1973 film *Blue Summer* is a heart-smart, funny, but also occasionally somber movie. Vincent has a thoroughly impressive filmography, including gems of both the Golden Age of Erotica (*Farewell Scarlett, Roommates, In Love*) and R-rated sex comedies (*Student Affairs, Cleo/Leo, Sex Appeal*). Out of his numerous directorial efforts, *Blue Summer* aka *The Love Truck* is one of the more obscure and wrongly so.

Being promoted as a trashy sexploitation film about "young bodies on the prowl" that "pay by the mile" didn't help matters. (As fantastically sleazy as that kind of byline is!) The film does have a healthy amount of sensuality with two protagonists fresh-outta-high-school having one last hurrah before going to college and adulthood. But this is Chuck Vincent at the helm, a man noted for incorporating characters with nuance and heart, often in film genres that "serious critics" typically don't give a second glance at.

In other words, *The Pigkeeper's Daughter* this ain't!

I know when I first saw it, back in the early 2000's, I went into it expecting some fun and low-grade/low-budget, trashy kitschy sleaze that only the 1970's could provide. What I got instead was a compelling story with two warm and relatable leads and a wise leadership from director/writer Vincent. There is plenty of nudity and roadside shenanigans for your more prurient desires, but this film's heart is bigger than its groin. For the most part.

The core of *Blue Summer* are best friends and overall good eggs Tracy (Darcey Hollingsworth aka Davey Jones) and Gene (Bo White). The film's opening frames begin in darkness that is quickly illuminated as Tracy opens the garage door at his parents' to get his newly festooned van out in preparation for their epic road trip to Stony Lake. True to life for an 18-year-old living at home from a lower-middle class family, Tracy's van looks like it has weathered at least a decade of dust and use. This is not a pimp van, though his attempts to make it one are charmingly low-rent. There's the crude sound system which is rigged together with wooden boards, a tape player and a loudspeaker roughly secured to the top of the roof. The real cherry on top is the van being resplendent with extremely 70's-style stickers of flowers, Mickey Mouse, and some white letters forming the vessel's newly christened name, "The Meat Wagon." Tracy's mom dotes on him before he leaves, even handing some extra "just in case" money, before yelling out while he starts to leave, "Tracy, what the hell did you do to that bus?!?"

In contrast to Tracy's sweet, though mildly concerned mom, Gene's parents come across, at best, horrible and at worst, future true crime fodder. In a cloud of second-hand chain smoke, his parents bitch and moan and nag. First at their son and then at each other. They are so absorbed in their dysfunctional cesspool that they don't even notice Gene grabbing the in-use coffee pot, toaster, and several bottles of strong-looking vodka. As he meets up with Tracy outside, he says, "Let's go! The shit's about to hit the fan!!" and then adds, "I hate the sight of blood!" as the air is littered with the house rockin' with domestic problems.

        The boys' toast with some cold, cheap brews, "Here's to incredible feats and chickies we meet!" (Drinking and driving were more casual in the 1970's. Just cue up some Bloodrock and a couple of cans of Hamm's and you're good to go!) Their journey is full of local color, including picking up some foxy runaways named Bea (Lilly Bi Peep, a one-time-wonder with a non-de-plume better suited for stag reels) and Sparky (Joann Sterling) with moxie-aplenty and sticky fingers. Girls in tow, they stop to help out a spooky biker (Jeff Allen), whom by the end of the movie ends up being the best guardian angel ripped on cheap speed and wearing swastika patches.

After the teenage grifters ditch the fellas for their new hosts/victims, the adventure continues. No matter what era you're living in, if you are road tripping through small town America, you will run into some religious kooks. Luckily for Tracy and Gene, the main one they pick up is a long-winded happy capitalist whose white suit matches his toothpaste smile. The good man is from the Tabernacle of the Holy Souls, who apparently were a precursor to The Church of Subgenius, since he asks for their ten dollar entrance fee for "...up there."

Speaking of shamen and charlatans, while changing a flat tire in a wooded area, the boys hear flute music. Following the notes, they stumble upon a long-haired guru flanked by two topless lovelies. He greets them with, "Welcome to my home. Let me introduce you to my women!" The man, whose name is the deliciously un-guru-like Roger (Larry Lima), initially declines their offer of beer but does accept their company and cigarettes. The flute plays on while the boys get friendly with redheaded Liza (Shana McGran) and dark-haired Deborah (Amy Mathieu). This scene is so warm and playful, with the four of them all kissing at the same time in a joint-group formation. The fact that Gene and Tracy are so comfortable with each other that there's zero need for pea-cocking or any "back off homo" bigot-alpha-male moves makes their friendship even more beautiful and admirable.

The realities of hanging out with a cult whose leader espouses philosophies, like "What's mine is yours and what's yours is mine" hit the boys pretty loud and clear soon after the fun. Being smart lads, though, they manage to comically break down their tent and gear around the comatose Roger and his girls. They sneak off, shaking themselves free of the worst kind of moochy hippies. The hangover of the flower power movement was none too pretty by 1973. Mercifully, the boys don't appear to suffer any further setbacks from Roger's girls, particularly of the creepy-crawly-itchy variety.

The next leg of their journey leads them to meet a good looking, golden-haired cool cat named Fred (Eric Edwards) at a no-name diner in a no-nothing town. Fred lets them know that the town is bereft of hot action, joking that the local women are locked up at sunset. Well, save for one. What follows is something that could very easily play out of a Charles Bukowski short story. Promising the boys that a local lady named Regina (Melissa Evers, who was also in the so bizarro it's good, must-see-midnight-oddity, 1975's *S.O.S. Screw on Screen*) will be hot to trot if they bring two cases of beer. So, the three of them show up at what has to be the shittiest looking garage/shack in recent film memory for this fateful encounter.

This Regina, who is the living, dripping definition of a blowsy blonde, is one class act. If by class, you mean reeking of cheap booze and snapping bon mots like, "I could dance all fucking night!" When she's not burping and badly dancing, she gets cranky with the boys and then proceeds to dance and more with a quite willing Fred. Gene and Tracy are resigned to tackle some sloppy seconds and thirds before a group of local rednecks show up for what can only be described as S.F. Brownrigg's Swinging Sex Party and bully the two boys out. Gene, thinking smarter not harder, makes sure to alert Regina's husband, who looks like the heftiest Bubba from the cast of Hee Haw, that something is going on in his ga-rage. Gunshots ensue, rednecks flee, and Regina may or may not be dead. You will not find that in your dog-eared copy of Fodor's travel guide.

The idyllic shores of Stony Lake are soon reached, with Tracy immediately off to locate an attractive, older woman whom he had given directions to back in town earlier in the film. He finds her small, white cottage and the two have a touching love scene that is tinged with pregnant dread. Even the instrumental music used is more melancholy compared to the rest of the film's more up-beat, rock-tinged score courtesy of an American band called Sleepy Hollow. Tracy's post-coital bliss is immediately hampered as the look of instant regret washes over his lover's face as she stammers about how she's never done anything like this before. It only gets worse as she insists on making lunch for him and after an excruciatingly awkward conversation, her son stops by. He and Tracy are clearly around the same age, with the latter leaving soon after.

While the grimmer aspects of adulthood are washing over poor Tracy, Gene is transfixed by a kooky, lithe blonde who keeps surprising him around the lake. The beauty refuses to give him her name or any personal details, resulting in Gene calling her Miss No Name (Chris Jordan, who was also married to Eric Edwards around this time). They make love with Gene clearly wanting to spend more time with her, only to be told that it's "not possible" before she runs off for good.

Driving back home, Tracy notes that "There'll be other summers!", but Gene knows better. "No. Not like this one." And he's right because once you're an adult, looking back is all you can do before moving forward. They toast to all of the characters they've met along the way, save for the two women of Stony Lake. The final toast is to school and freedom, with the van becoming quiet as our two men look sad and glumly resigned to a future that feels like it is already not purely their own to claim.

This film and that ending are sad-eyed gold. The themes of adult-reality and sacrificing personal freedom and will permeate throughout. The boys are going to different colleges, all due to having to attend their fathers' alma mater. Both of them are clearly not ready for college, but have acquiesced to the familial pressure of "this is what you have to do." There are adults all around them who have made a mess of their lives. Gene's parents are miserable as hell, Regina's probably dead, and Tracy's older lover is trapped and neglected in a loveless marriage that she sees no way out of. The one big exception is the biker, who just creeps, drifts, and then commits acts of surprise heroism. Tracy and Gene's fates are up in the air, leaving the audience with the thin hope that the two will see outside their parents status quo-expectations prison.

If *The Pom Pom Girls* is a light slice of 70's teenage-life and *Blue Summer* is a fun but melancholy last gasp of coming-of-age, then 1982's *The Last American Virgin* is a stylish, emotional gut-punch whose reverb remains heart-strong long after you finished watching it. If you told a bunch of cineastes at a party that *The Last American Virgin* has a similar poignant and devastating effect of something like most of the John

Cassavetes' catalog, you may get some quizzical looks or even worse, derisive snorts. They can shuffle right off because they are wrong. It was promoted as another wacky teenage-sex-comedy with a killer soundtrack, which featured The Cars, The Gleaming Spires (a tremendously underrated band), The Police, The Plimsouls, Devo, just to name a few. (Seriously, this movie is so good that it makes REO Speedwagon's Sears Roebuck schmaltz hit, "Keep on Loving You" work. That is borderline cinematic witchcraft.)

So on one hand, sure, *The Last American Virgin* fits that bill. There are themes of sex and virginity, paired with a kicky soundtrack. But it is also one of the rawest and most honest films about being a teenager ever made. It's right next to *Over the Edge* (1979) and Rene Daalder's *Massacre at Central High* (1976) when it comes to masterfully made films that deal with the harsher realities of growing up in post-Vietnam America. Ironically, all three of the above were directed by men who are not from the United States. *The Last American Virgin* was helmed by Boaz Davidson, who was born in Tel Aviv. Davidson first came to prominence with his 1978 film, *Lemon Popsicle*. Set in 1950's Israel and based on some of Davidson's real-life experiences growing up, *Lemon Popsicle* was a massive hit and would go on to have eight, count'em, eight sequels.

It was so successful, that it would go on to net its own remake in America, thanks to the great Menahem Golan and Yoram Globus over at Cannon Films. The Go-Go Boys are partially to thank for *The Last American Virgin* getting made! Getting Davidson to write and direct it? Even better.

In lesser hands, this would have been weakened considerably, but Davidson took his equally great original and used it to create something with equal heart, honesty, and a few more rows of sharp teeth. The golden-hued nostalgia of *Lemon Popsicle* is replaced with some keen-eyed Western cynicism sinking into nihilism.

Put your seatbelts on, because this is going to be a heartbreaker.

The film focuses on Gary (Lawrence Monoson). When he's not delivering pizzas for The Pink Pizza, Gary is hanging out with his friends, cocky Rick (Steve Antin) and goofy David (Joe Rubbo, who really should have been in more movies). Like typical high schoolers hopped up on hormones and a little bit of fear, they spend their days and nights in the hopes of getting laid. But a wrench is thrown into the plan when he meets Karen (cult darling Diane Franklin). Johnny Thunders once warned not to mess with cupid, but Gary is already doomed. He manages to net giving her a ride to school, via him letting the air out of her bike's tire. Gary gets the gumption to ask her out to a party later that night. She gives him a polite brush-off, saying she already has "plans."

Fate is the cruelest mistress, which Gary quickly learns as he sees Karen at said party, dancing with Rick and looking like the smittenest kitten. Rick is the same guy whom earlier in the film, responded to one girl telling him, pre-coitus, that she "wasn't on the pill" with that he wasn't either. In other words, this is not going to end well. Gary handles this like any of us would at 17/18 (or 35/36), by getting instantly shitfaced at the party, to the extent of worrying your one actually decent friend (that would be non-jabroni, David) and horrifying your parents.

The next day, the boys have an amusing interlude with an older, hot-to-trot pizza customer named Carmela (the always vivacious Louisa Moritz), that results in Rick and then David getting to bed her. Before Gary can sample the giving woman, her BIG boyfriend, Paco, comes home! The guys escape and unlike *Blue Summer*, the likelihood of murder seems pretty minimal. One cute touch is how scared David looks before getting seduced by Carmela, which Rubbo pulls off magnificently. For every cocksure Rick in the bunch, there are going to be a lot more David and Garys in this world.

Rick manages to not only con Gary in going on a double date, since Karen doesn't want to go out unless her bespectacled, mega-babe friend Rose (Kimmy "Motherfucking" Robertson) tags along, but also poor, nerdy Victor (Scuz himself, Brian Peck) into lending them his vintage convertible Pontiac. After Gary has the awful experience of having to see the girl of his dreams neck with his buddy, beachside, Victor's car ends up crashing into the ocean. (Jesus, maybe Victor's the real bad luck Barney in this movie.)

Gary does manage to cockblock Rick, who was looking at borrowing Gary's grandmother's house to have some "alone time" with Karen. David and Gary both manage to tease Rick about "playing house" with Karen, while they brag about going to see a big breasted hooker named Ruby (Nancy Brock). Rick gets jealous and breaks his date with Karen to go with his buddies.

The movie up to this point has already had some good foreshadowing to the inevitable tragedy, right up to the party near the beginning playing "Better Luck Next Time" by Oingo Boingo. But this is where the big ugly is going to come in. Ruby is no hooker with a heart of gold but instead is a hard-bitten streetwalker whose very aura reeks of bad decisions, rough breaks, and Pall Malls. After securing the money, she takes them inside a grimy looking warehouse. Gary, who is clearly still a virgin, gets to have his introduction to lovemaking on a dirty couch with a woman barking at him to "Get those pants off!" The encounter is mercifully short but leaves him vomiting off to the side while David goes next. The fact that this leaves all of them with an infestation of crabs makes the whole proceeding especially horrid. But you know what else is horrid? Real life.

When trying to drown their new parasitic little buddies in the public pool does not work, the three of them go to a drug store where Gary manages to bumble his way to ask for the proper medication. Luckily they don't live in the Bible Belt and the gregarious pharmacist laughs and helps them out. But crabs are just the tip of the iceberg when it comes the dangers of unprotected sex.

Gary shows up at the usual diner, seeing Karen's bicycle outside. But there's no Karen, or Rick, for that matter, inside. Victor lets it slip that he saw the

two of them head off to the football stadium. Being a heart-sick fool, Gary goes over there, only to find his "best friend" about to deflower an unsure but ultimately willing Karen. The night only gets worse when his buddy finds him back at the diner, telling him that "I was the first one to get Miss Thing over there. I fucked Karen!", while she is ordering some ice cream. Keeping it classy, Rick. Gary doesn't handle this well and drives off, to the sad tune of "Just Once" by Quincy Jones. The refrain of "I did my best, but my best wasn't good enough" is going to haunt young Gary throughout the rest of this movie.

Rick's lack of fondness for condoms or common human decency catches up to him, as Gary sees him give Karen a nasty brush off in the school library. He goes to comfort her while she is crying by her locker. She reveals that she's pregnant and though he is taken aback, he immediately tells her that everything is going to be okay and he is going to take care of it. Gary confronts Rick, who is, quelle surprise, an asshole, and the two almost come to blows.

Utilizing a school ski trip as a perfect guise, Gary sets Karen up at his late grandmother's house. He also goes with her to get her abortion arranged. Anyone that assumes that getting an abortion is a breezy thing, especially in 1982 (or 2018), should see this movie. The woman at the clinic is cold and blatantly judgmental, especially to Karen, who is clearly young and scared. This leads to one exquisite montage. Clean edits juxtapose Gary hustling to get the money to pay for Karen's abortion, while she is crying and undressing, all set to U2's "I Will Follow."

"A boy tries hard to be a man/His mother takes him by his hand/If he stops to think he starts to cry/Oh why."

The way Karen is being handled there is further emphasized by one shot of her going under that quick cuts to a close-up of a pizza being sliced. Bedside manner is something a lot of women and girls don't get when it comes to their bodies. Gary goes to pick her up, bringing her a gift of a bag of oranges and a small Christmas tree, which is such a sweet and dorky touch. He gets to platonically play house with Karen while she rests up. She lets him know how much she appreciates him, calling him a "true friend." He breaks down and tells her that he loves her. God, Lawrence Monoson is just pure emotion here. Naked vulnerability just pours out of him. He finally gets to kiss and hug the girl of his dreams.

Getting ready for her upcoming birthday party, he buys her golden heart locket, complete with a personalized inscription. The Plimsouls "Zero Hour" plays as he shows up to the party.

"It's getting late, now it's time to go/It's over the top now, it's out of control/Just a matter of time 'til the zero hour."

Zero hour indeed, because the preciousness of life and heart is something that can be completely altered in one moment. A twist of fate can murder your optimism and tear your heart to shreds. Gary goes looking for Karen, only to find her back in Rick's arms in the kitchen. The quiet devastation that washes over him is beyond visceral. He then drives off into the night, tears running down his face as that goddamned Quincy Jones song plays again.

For anyone who has ever had their heart broken and gotten caught in a dream that quickly died, which really should be anyone who has a pulse and a not-totally-corroded heart, the slings and arrows Gary weathers hit so close to home. The unflinching honesty that Davidson gives us here is not needlessly cruel or exploitative, but instead is coming from someone who truly cares. A real artist/friend/lover will be real with you and real is exactly what you end up getting with this film.

Cinching all of this is the young cast, who are all absolutely perfect here, with the two sides of the coin being Monoson and Diane Franklin. Monoson nails his character so hard, making his pain wholly tangible. It's mind-blowing to know that this was both his and Franklin's first major film acting roles. Franklin is radiant as the sweet but intensely naive Karen. Side note, but I once actually got in a minor online debate over this movie, in particular, the actions of Karen. Listen, don't be dumb like me. Your morning constitutional is infinitely more healthy and rewarding than arguing with ANYONE over the net. But there was some callousness about her ending up back with Rick. Is it a dumb decision? Yes. Is it a ridiculously bad decision. Absolutely but anyone who didn't make some ill thought out, impulsive decisions, especially in their late teens is either a robot or lying or a lying robot. That's part of the fabric of human pain is that we as a species can make some poor choices that are rooted in being blinded by our heart and loins. It happens and if one wants perfection in their fictional teens, then go watch the Disney Channel and keep living in that sanitized bubble.

In addition to having some airtight acting, writing, music, and directing, the film's cinematography and art direction are especially striking. There are repeated tones and hues of bubblegum pinks, baby blues, and bright yellows, giving the inevitable death march of Gary's dream and love a deceptive candy-like sheen.

Growing into the sea-legs of adulthood is never easy and while it's not all agony and letdowns, it is also not all good times and rebellion either. It's a spicy gumbo and when a film can nail any of that in a way that is both sincere and different like these three films do, then you know that you truly have something special. At the end of the day, we may be beaten, but we are never ever broken.

RAISED WITH A FILM BOOK IN HER HANDS, HEATHER DRAIN HAS BEEN CAPTIVATED BY THE LANGUAGE OF CINEMA SINCE DAY ONE. BORN AND RAISED IN ARKANSAS, SHE WENT FROM WRITING LEONARD MALTIN STYLED REVIEWS OF TITLES RANGING FROM **CEMETERY HIGH** TO **WOMEN ON THE VERGE OF A NERVOUS BREAKDOWN** IN THE FIFTH GRADE TO WRITING FOR PUBLICATIONS LIKE **VIDEO WATCHDOG, THE EXPLOITATION JOURNAL, LUNCHMEAT, ART DECADES, CASHIERS DU CINEMART, SCREEM** AND **THE LITTLE ROCK FREE PRESS** SEVERAL YEARS LATER. SHE HAS ALSO BEEN A CONTRIBUTOR TO **DANGEROUS MINDS, DIABOLIQUE, THE RIALTO REPORT, PARACINEMA, CINEMA HEAD CHEESE, CULTCUTS** AND, ON OCCASION, AS A GUEST WRITER, OVER AT BOTH **RUPERT PUPKIN SPEAKS** AND TURNER CLASSIC'S **MOVIE MORLOCKS** BLOG.

SHE LIVES WITH HER PAINTER/WRITER HUSBAND, C.F. ROBERTS AND THEIR TWO WONDERFUL AND SEMI-SURLY RESCUE CATS, ZIGGY AND TALLULAH. FROM MONDOHEATHER.COM

A CONVERSATION WITH STOYA

by Jeremy R. Richey

Still from STOYA PICTURE PERFECT
(Digital Playground, 2008)

Behind the scenes photos by Kelley Avery

EARLIER THIS YEAR I HAD THE GREAT PRIVILEGE TO SIT DOWN WITH ACTRESS, ARTIST, FILMMAKER, PROVOCATEUR AND WRITER STOYA FOR AN IN DEPTH CONVERSATION ABOUT HER CAREER WITH A SPECIAL FOCUS ON HER WRITING. WE MET IN THE LOBBY OF A DENVER, COLORADO HOTEL BEFORE THE 2018 XXXOTICA EXPO, WHERE STOYA WAS APPEARING VIA A NUMBER OF SEMINARS. SINCE APPEARING ON THE SCENE AS AN UNFORGETTABLE ADULT ACTRESS IN 2006, STOYA HAS PROVEN HERSELF TO BE ONE OF THE MOST INTELLIGENT AND TALENTED FIGURES IN POPULAR AMERICAN CULTURE. HER WORK HAS RAN THE SPECTRUM FROM WRITING FOR SOME OF THE MOST RESPECTED PUBLICATIONS IN THE COUNTRY, WINNING ACCLAIM AND AWARDS FOR HER PERFORMANCES IN BOTH ADULT AND MAINSTREAM FILMS, DIRECTING HER OWN PROJECTS, POD-CASTING AND EVEN THEATRICAL WORK. IN JUST OVER A DECADE, STOYA'S RESUME IS ALREADY MORE DIVERSE THAN
MOST ARTISTS CAN EVEN DREAM OF.
IT WAS A REAL PLEASURE DISCUSSING HER CAREER WITH HER
AND I CAN'T THANK HER ENOUGH FOR HER
KINDNESS AND TIME.

SOLEDAD: Thanks so much for sitting down for this Stoya. I wanted to mainly concentrate on your writing so to begin with what was the first publication you wrote for?

STOYA: It was a comment piece for *The Guardian*. It was my first professional piece

Have you always been interested in writing?

When I was a kid I wanted to be a dancer and if somebody pushed for a backup I would have said journalism. I started writing first like blogs, which were part of social media in a way, then I started writing things seriously because I felt like journalists were leaving important things out that the general public just wouldn't understand.

Do you still do some blogging?

Sometimes, but when I'm working on professional pieces then I don't blog as much or at all.

Do you approach blogging and professional pieces different?

It depends how much editing there is. I do really well with structure edits, or rather sometimes I need structure edits, and that can entirely change where you want to take the second half of the piece. Where you are basically writing from scratch, at least the second half.

What has your experience been with different editors like?

M y experience overall has been more positive mostly because I'm working with editors for 2nd or 3rd time. I've found good ones and I stick with them.

Were there a lot of books around your house when you were growing up?

There were definitely a lot of books around my whole life. It's really great now that electronic devices that can hold lots of books because that makes moving easier and cuts down on a wall of books.

How was your Verge column Ask Stoya different than your other writing?

So I had done an advice column in the past and questions usually required a little more research. Instead of giving my opinion, or my view on something, it was largely 'here are some options to think about' so the structure was different. Something that I found interesting was that with each publication the questions at the end would become about the same thing like "my partner and I want to have a slightly open thing and how do we navigate that?" I just found that sort of odd.

Have you ever felt Pigeonholed with your writing?

I'm largely interested in pornography and sexuality and I can see how a different performer might feel pigeonholed but that's what I'm in interested in covering. I have this video series, *Around The World In 80 Ways,* that is like a parody of parachute journalism where it's like "I'm here and here's that wacky sex thing and then it's like lets talk about communism for a second!" but with my writing I try and stay away from things I don't know about and I specialize so much in sex.

Has your writing or subject matter changed at all since Trump got elected?

I'm sort of insulated because my assistant handles social media. I'm in a fairly unique position because I live in New York and know people who sort of make the news or who cover important chunks of things. I don't even look at a newspaper very often. I'm like 'is there anything I have to know about right now?'   'No...okay great.' I'll ask my roommate if there is anything critical then I'll look it up.

You spend a lot of time out of the States. Are perceptions about you and your work different around the world?

Mostly I spend time in Serbia lately. It's weird because I am held to a different standard because I'm foreign and because I was already notable by the time they became aware of me. Then I did that science fiction film, *Ederlezi Rising,* that was very well received by critics and festival audiences.

You won a major award at the
FEST INTERNATIONAL FILM FESTIVAL
for that didn't you?

Best actress, it was an honor.

How did the film come about.

My friend Nicola, a photographer who photographed me at 18 or 19. He emailed me one day and said 'some of my friends from school are making a science fiction film in Serbia' and I was like "I'm there"! They sent over a treatment and it was very good. It was very precise and I was like 'I'm definitely in'. It took awhile to secure funding, like a number years.
We shot it at the end of 2015 then we had to wait a little bit for all the post production and CGI.

What are your thoughts on feminism and the Me Too movement?

I think for women in general there's a raised awareness of how bad the situation is and that can be a good first step. I respect what a lot of women who identify as feminist have done.
I get uncomfortable when people try to apply the term to my work but the short of it is that
while a lot of my beliefs are feminist
I'm not making them explicit in my pornographic work
so its inappropriate to use that word to describe it.

I'm definitely the director and handle the production. That's everything from funding to wrangling the paperwork. Wolf Hudson has done some of the editing and I perform, operate the camera and direct.

Would you be interested in directing a Feature length film at some point?

I would love to make good narrative stuff happen but I don't know if I need to direct it. I might be perfectly happen in production.

Do you think we'll ever see a return to the classic narrative driven adult films of the seventies?

I don't think it's going to be like a feature movie anymore. It's going to be episodic or a one off with two scenes. I saw one recently where it was a like a movies worth of narrative with two sex scenes. It was really good and it served the basic function of pornography but it also had a really compelling narrative. It was only 45 minutes and I think if they tried to do an hour and a half they would have had to add a side plot, that would have been better as its own, or stretch out sex scenes that would have just been fast forwarded through and affected the pacing.

Were there any films you did with Digital Playground that you found more interesting than others?

Not really. They did stuff that had incredible production qualities but the narratives weren't very interesting.

I love your Vice article, Art is Just as Powerful as Protest? What are your thoughts on how much more active younger people seem to be politically and protest wise?

As far as kid's awareness being raised...as long as it comes with critical thinking and the understanding we're going to need options to have a better plan in place. So that we don't need to be afraid if someone like Trump gets elected again. I think kids being aware is really great.

Tell us a bit about the play you were recently in The Last Bar At the End of the World?

It is Dean Haspiel's third play and second one I'm doing with him. It's an existential noir about a dying comic book artist. I play a very quirky women on the subway. I really like it, it's super fun. I did a lot of ballet as a kid so I'm good at emoting.

Thanks so much Stoya for taking time out of your busy schedule to do this. It was an honor and I greatly appreciate it.

As we were wrapping up I presented Stoya with a copy of Art Decades Issue 5 because it featured our tribute to the late great Candida Royalle, whom I knew she greatly admired, to which Stoya excitedly replied,

Candida was a hero!

To Which I thought Candida certainly has a great spiritual heir.

STOYA IN PRINT

Earlier this year Not A Cult media released Stoya's first book *Philosophy, Pussycats, & Porn*, a terrific near 200 page paperback volume of her collected works. *Philosophy, Pussycats, & Porn* features dozens of informative, insightful and often moving essays by Stoya including a number of her previously published works from outlets like *The New York Times*, *Dazed* and *Hustler*. It's not a 'compete works' collection, as it doesn't include a number of her important online and printed pieces from the past several years, but it is an excellent book that is an essential read for both seasoned fans and interested newcomers. Illustrated throughout with a number of provocative sketches, *Philosophy, Pussycats, & Porn*'s subject matter runs the gamut from sex to politics to deeply personal pieces. Throughout the book, Stoya shows that she is one of modern popular culture's most intriguing thinkers and vibrant personalities. Her voice is strong, her writing style sharp and compulsively readable, and her subject matter is sometimes confrontational and always unflinchingly honest. *Philosophy, Pussycats, & Porn* is one of the best books of 2018 and more information on it can be found at notacult.media/books/pussycats.

Three more older, but no less essential, publications are well worth seeking out for those interested in Stoya and her work. Copies of the fifth issue of the gorgeous coffee table book quality *Richardson* magazine, featuring an interview with cover star Stoya along with a startling photo essay by legendary Steven Klein, are still available at https://richardsonshop.com/collections/magazines/products/richardson-a5 although each issue of *Richardson* typically sells out eventually so followers who don't already have a copy should make haste. Copies of the issue also come with a poster of the striking Klein cover, featuring Stoya in one of her fiercest and most iconic shots.

Sadly the two Bad Book LTD books featuring Stoya, *Troll Witch* and *Stoya Team Rockstar* are currently out of print. I was fortunate enough to snag *Stoya Team Rock Star* upon its release and it's a wonderful photo collection featuring Stoya captured by photographer Steve Prue on instant Fuji instax film. *Stoya Team Rockstar* feels like a printed road movie and it's quite delightful...imagine vintage Wim Wenders with nudity. Samples can still be seen at badbooksltd.com/store/stoya-x-team-rockstar, although the only planned printing was the initial run of 500.

Troll Witch is described by Stoya at Bad Book LTD's website with ""For over a decade, my work was hardcore sex scenes but my main medium of expression was essentially real-time social media. Over the course of three days in Spring 2016 I stopped filtering myself before tweeting. This book is selections form those tweets." Featuring 'words, watercolor, magic marker, and portraiture. and original artwork by Stoya and portraits by Steve Prue', *Troll Witch* was also limited to just 500 copies. Samples can still be seen as well at badbooksltd.com/store/troll-witch.

Stoya has, of course, also been featured in numerous pictorials throughout the years in a variety of publications and a number of always insightful interviews are available out there as well. Hopefully a companion volume to *Philosophy, Pussycats, & Porn* might one day appear that collects more of Stoya's work but for now happy hunting!

-Jeremy R. Richey-

Follow Stoya and her work at:

twitter.com/stoya
zerospaces.com/ (NSFW)
instagram.com/stoya/
facebook.com/ederlezirisingoffical/
trenchcoatx.com/series/around-the-world-in-80-ways.html (NSFW)

Fires
Les Bohem

"Someone like you should not be allowed to start any fires."
David Bowie "Win"

My friend Peter Woolcott was incredibly good-looking. The great grandson
of a duke, he had the classic features of a prince, with a combination of
arrogance and vulnerability that was amazingly appealing. Peter's good
looks had not given him that irritating sort of self-confidence that is the
distinguishing mark of most attractive people. He was prone to fruitless
introspection, very much afraid of saying the wrong thing, and I think
that there was something in his personality that clouded his sight
whenever he took a look at his own reflection.

Peter was something of a dabbler. At twenty-seven he had already
painted, photographed, sculpted, tried for rock stardom, renounced the
material world in search of self, and taken up back-packing. He was not
oblivious to the state of his wandering ambitions although, in his more
positive moods, he did take a certain pride in his inability to settle down.
Unlike most dabblers, he seemed to be good at whatever he attempted. I
always felt that he was at the most a month away from producing a
masterpiece.

Peter and I had been roommates in an apartment in NoHo for about six
months when we were both twenty-one. Many of our evenings were spent with
a bottle of tequila, drinking our way through the suddenly ancient
histories of our adolescence. I think it was the first time that either of
us were really aware of the intangible reality of the past, or aware that
we had one.

Peter's life had been shaped by his romances. Peter had an absolute faith
in love. He truly believed that somewhere in that magic concept lay the
answer to all his problems; that if he could just find his other half, the
world would fall neatly into place. He clung to his memories with a
passion. In high school, his world had revolved around a girl named
Debbie. She never liked him, preferring a string of UCLA theatre majors
with full beards and deep expressions. She did, however, spend the night
with him in a sleeping bag at the Renaissance Faire at the Santa Fe Dam.
When he called her, she was disquietingly friendly, and a short while
later she married their biology teacher. Peter carved her number on the
inside door of his bedroom closet and swore never to forget her.

Just before we'd moved into the apartment in North Hollywood, Peter had
lived with a girl named Diane. He would talk for hours about how
happy they had been until something restless in him had gained control
and made him throw away his chance. Peter was afraid that Diane had been
his golden moment, that he had left his destiny in her Toyota station
wagon in the Ralph's parking lot at Curson and Sunset where he had told
her that he thought that they should see other people. He still followed
her Instagram, sulking every time she posted a photograph of the dinner
she'd just had and the boy who'd bought it for her.

As I said, Peter and I lived together for about six months. Then he moved
to Silverlake. He had begun to paint. I went to several of his shows, and
we had an occasional drink together, but all our meetings were in crowds.

Peter was changing in a disturbing way. Like most romantics, he was
strikingly selfish, and his narcissism had left him in a precarious
balance. He was at once conceited and insecure, and this combination had
begun to produce a self-hatred that could only lead to his own
destruction.

Peter himself seemed all too aware of the machinery of this, but
unwilling to move out of its way. While still chasing his notions of
idealized love, Peter forced himself into the most unromantic situations
conceivable. With a friend of his named Charles, he visited paid admission
"parties" in the Hollywood Hills where roomfuls of naked men and women
writhed and sweated in a ritual of total anonymity. It was as if some
terrible revulsion drove him further and further away from himself, while
at the same time he proved to himself that he could get the best of a world
he totally despised.

About two years ago, Peter started a photography studio in West Hollywood
with a friend of his from school. Like all his other attempts, his
photographs were wonderful. He had an eye that wouldn't miss; he was
unerring in his ability to find the visual expression of an emotion. But
there was something disturbing in the photographs, just as there was in
the zeal with which he had thrown himself into his latest means of
expression. A smugness had come over Peter since he'd started taking
pictures, as if capturing isolated moments -- a pretense of reality-had
given him some bizarre grant of power. You felt this in his images; there
was a confinement there, a very real sense of boundary. His subjects were
his prisoners. After looking at the pictures, I had the definite feeling
that Peter had brought himself to the brink of imminent disaster.

It was over a year after Peter had started the studio that he called me
one Saturday night and asked me to pick him up. We had not seen each other
once in that time. There was an urgency in his voice that was almost fear.
He was staying in Laurel Canyon with his friend, Charles. Several months
before, Charles had married into rock and roll aristocracy. His wife was
Andrea Moon whose beautiful face was even then smiling down onto the
Sunset Strip from an enormous billboard. Her album had gone platinum the
week that she and Charles met, and she was coasting now on what seemed to
be a never-ending stream of hit singles. They lived together in a palace
hat had been built for a silent film star. Charles was a stylish, vicious
boy of twenty-five who snorted too much coke and drank himself into
oblivion at the Soho nearly every night. He and Peter had known each
other for years, and Peter, while repulsed, was drawn again and again into
his company, perhaps envying a road to annihilation that was so direct.

It was raining heavily and the canyon was an unfriendly blur. I parked
up the street from the house and walked past a waiting limousine. The
driver was inside reading on his phone, encased in his little shell of
light with too much clarity, like something extinct on display in a
museum.

Charles answered the door dressed in a maroon robe. He had a glass of wine
in his hand and looked as if he had just woken up. He was anxious to show
the house off, taking me from room to room and telling me little snatches
of the place's history. "Some old star, I think her name was Mabel Desmond
or something, she broke her leg sliding down this banister."

 As we continued our tour, Charles moved to the present, convinced that
 anyone would be fascinated with the details of his newly acquired status.

He spoke completely in the plural, making a point of establishing that "we" were putting in a new recording studio downstairs because "we" had taken over our own management and as a result "our" finances were greatly improved. "We're monitoring the downloads on all platforms, and I'm negotiating a preferred rate from Spotify so we don't get raped there." What struck me most about the house was not its enormous size or its structure, but the unbelievable disinterest with which it had been decorated. There were none of the garish deco excesses that had probably been the original furnishings, or any of the ultra-modern vulgarities that might have been expected to replace them. It was as if Charles and Andrea Moon had gone into a furniture store and, blindfolded, had bought just enough to fill the rooms of their new house.

Peter met us upstairs. He was just coming out of the shower. I had forgotten how handsome he was. He disappeared into one of the bedrooms and Charles and I went down two flights of stairs to the game room and the as yet unfinished recording studio.

Andrea Moon was in the game room, sunken into a brown Naugahyde couch, watching a rerun of Friends on a huge monitor. The aspect ratio hadn't been adjusted on the TV and the actors looked squat and misshapen. The sound was up so loud that the speakers were distorting. Between Andrea and the monitor were scattered a half-dozen boxes of Colonel Sanders chicken, filled with half-eaten pieces. There were empty coke cans littered around them. No lights were on, so that the room went black occasionally when the image on the monitor darkened. Charles introduced us and Andrea turned and smiled. She had a Japanese robe thrown on and, as she turned, the robe dropped to her waist. Her body, reflected in the light from the monitor was something wild and foreign. It was as if, having sat down to dinner in a restaurant, you turned to see a sleek young leopard stalking between the tables. The room went dark and then a commercial came on and she was facing the set, the robe pulled back over her shoulders. She leaned forward and picked through the boxes for a piece of cold chicken.

We moved towards the window and Charles reached for a handgun that was sitting on the ledge. It was a small gun, about the length of a paperback book, but with a thick barrel a yard long that stuck out from it in an unnatural way as if it been put there by mistake. Charles handed the gun to me with a grim smile. "Seven point six two millimeter," he said. "A Madsen. I do my own loads, fifteen grain, steel jacket over lead. It'll do over 1500 rounds a minute. In Nam they called that rock and roll."

He took it back from me and pulled off the long grey tube. "The silencer is the barrel," he said, pushing the barrel back into place and pointing it vaguely out the window. "I could turn that chauffeur to runny garbage; but it's really made for close range. I've got an Uzi I keep upstairs by the window. I got them from a guy."

He nodded back over his shoulder at his wife. " A lot of heavy people are into Andrea," he said; "and we stepped on a lot of toes with the management trip. We make a lot of money." He lowered his voice dramatically. "Russians," he said proudly and put the gun back on the window ledge.

Peter had come downstairs. Charles wanted us to stay, but Peter made our excuses. Andrea turned away from the monitor and looked up at us. Again, for a moment, I had the feeling of something animal looking out from her eyes. "Come back soon," she said.

"I had to get out of there," Peter said as we walked to the car. "Thanks."
"I thought you were living in Hollywood," I said.
"I'll tell you about it. I've got to pick up some clothes. Do you mind? It's on the way."
We drove down the Canyon in an uncomfortable silence. Peter was distracted, bursting, but not yet ready to tell me about it. Instead, we started to talk about Charles. "I've known him for so long that to me, he's playing at it," Peter said. "Just a kid playing gangster. But maybe that's all it is for anyone. I mean, he 's done some things that touch real people."
"What happens if Andrea dumps him?"
"Andrea s not like us. I mean, a year ago she was taking a bus up from Huntington Park to clean houses. It's an accident of modern life that their worlds ever overlapped."
We went to a duplex on Havenhurst just below Fountain. It was Spanish, tan, with a dead lawn and peeling paint.
"This'll be kind of weird," Peter said. "Do you mind coming in?"
We crossed the street and went in. A stairway led to the door to the upstairs apartment. As we started up as, we were met by a series of horrible noises followed by a woman's voice, hoarse and ugly.
"Bitches, you're all manufactured. Someone has to beat the world back into you."
The door opened into a large living room. All the furniture had been pushed to the walls; the carpet had been rolled to one side. The room was long to begin with and the effect now was one of dream-like distortion. Against the far wall, nearly obscured by the furniture, were several canvases and a series of framed photographs that I recognized as Peter's. There were six women in the room, all dressed in leotards. One, with a shock of wild brown hair, stood, facing the others, her back to us.
"There's nothing real in any of your lives," she screamed at the other women. Hers was the gruff voice we'd heard from the stairs.
The women's attention had wandered to the doorway where we stood. The shock of hair woman turned and looked at us. She wore bright lipstick and no other make-up. Her face was pock-marked.
"God damn it," she said.
One of the others, the prettiest, her hair short and very red, looked over at us with a terribly angry glare.
"Excuse us," Peter said in a loud, self-conscious voice. He turned back down the hallway and went into one of the bedrooms. I followed uncomfortably. He turned on a light and started to pick through a pile of clothes on an unmade bed.
"I told you it'd be weird," he said. There were angry footsteps in the hall and the red-head stood in the doorway.
"What the hell are you doing, Peter?" she asked. Her lower lip trembled, which is something I had only seen in a movie, "You know Goddamned well my group is rehearsing, I thought we'd agreed that you would stay out of here. You're like some kind of bad child." She stared at him, and her eyes were actually getting wet. He didn't answer.
"It's atmosphere, you stupid bastard, you ruined the atmosphere. "
"This is my friend," Peter said, introducing me. "This is Calley, my wife."
I was surprised, and I'm sure I showed it.
Calley turned to me. "Hello," she said and offered her hand. She had a strong, dry handshake. "We do plays here. Last summer we did Ibsen, now

we're doing something contemporary. John Spencer. Do you know him?"
I shook my head slightly. Peter's wife. There was such a formal permanence
to that. It was so very grown up. Up close, Calley was not really that
pretty. She had one of those faces that seemed to fall into its separate
pieces, very big teeth and a slightly crooked nose. Her lips just a little
too thin. But then, as you stared, all the parts fit back together and her
face became alive and wonderful. There was something familiar to me about
her, something that disturbed me. I tried to hide my staring behind
conversation.
"Spencer?" I said. "Is he from LA?"
She was fairly tall and very thin and she carried herself with a
sophistication that was effective even though it was transparently
self-conscious. She wore her leotard as if it were straight out of Paris
Vogue.
"No one knows much about him. This play is based on St. Augustine's
Confessions. It's very real."
Her most startling feature was her eyes. They were jet black. "Augustine?" I
said. Suddenly I understood the familiarity. I had seen her several years
before, in Peter's paintings. Paintings he'd done long before he'd met her.
Peter had finally found his masterpiece. It was as if she were his own
creation.
"Let's take a break," the gruff voice screamed from the living room. "Who
wants to be the first to kiss and get nasty?"
 "Rhonda is a wild woman," Calley said without smiling at all.
Peter had been watching us intently, and I realized that Calley had been
deliberately ignoring him, playing me neatly in between them as we talked.
"All right then," he said; "I just came to get a shirt." He had taken off his
old shirt and was replacing it with one that looked just as dirty. "Let's
go," he said to me.
Calley turned and looked at him with stage sadness. "Will you be back
tonight?" she asked.
My presence was making Peter uncomfortable. He shuffled through his
dirty clothes on the bed.
"You know how I am when I'm working," she went on.   "Things get so
difficult. You understand."
Peter winced. He said that he did understand. That he did know.
"I love him," Calley said to me. "He doesn't believe that I do, but I love him."
I didn't say anything and she turned back to Peter.
"Are you still staying up at Charles', then?" she asked. Peter looked up at
her and then turned back to the clothes.
"All right," she said. "I don't know. I'm a bitch," She walked out of the room.
Went back to her rehearsal.
For a moment, I thought Peter would run after her, but he just stood and he
said, "Let's get a drink." We started out the door and got to the bottom of
the stairs. "Would you mind waiting a minute?" he asked and ran back up.
I stepped outside and waited. In about ten minutes, Peter came back down.
His eyes were red and there was a distance in them; he was caught by
something that he didn't understand.

We went to a bar on Third Street and drank bourbon like a couple of hard
guys in an old movie. Once he started, Peter spoke in an explosion of
confused frustration. He talked straight through me as if I weren't there

at all. He had met Calley a little over a year ago at a party. She had been standing by the punch bowl pouring a drink for a middle-aged man with long hair and French jeans. She was smiling and she looked drunk. She spilled a little punch on the man's hands and she laughed; then she looked up and caught Peter staring. He wet over to the punch bowl for a refill. "And you've seen her," he said, looking for her reflection in his shot glass. "She was wearing a black dress. She looked wonderful."

They started seeing each other regularly. Calley was four years older than Peter. She was living in the apartment on Havenhurst with her six year old son, Justin. Justin's father was a fairly successful songwriter who had just released his first album. He and Calley had lived together in Echo Park for eight years. One day, having signed a recording contract, he had come home, packed his things in a cardboard box, and moved to Beverly Glen. His album had been hailed by Rolling Stone as the greatest west coast debut since Jackson Browne, a work rich in sensitivity and insight. Justin had been five and Calley twenty-eight.

Calley and Peter had problems right from the start. With her twenties virtually over, Calley had begun to panic as the promise of success faded gradually from a destination to an impossibility, until her growing desperation became the focal point of their relationship. She would go into black periods in which Peter became her persecuting demon, a heartless bastard whose selfishness was holding her back. She was jealous of everything that was his; his paintings, his age, even his sadness, which was pure an untroubled by ambition.

Peter moved into Calley's apartment two months after they met. He was out of his head in love with her.

"We spent nearly all of our time fighting. I don't know, maybe I am selfish. We'd fight all the time, right up to the last moment; but then, Jesus, making love is like nothing I've ever known. It's like fire."

"What about the kid?"

"He's real nice. A little messed up and kind of quiet. I'm painting again. I did a painting of him, but you couldn't see it tonight."

"Where was he tonight?"

"At Calley's mom's. He spends a lot of time there."

"When did you get married?"

"It was about six months ago. We had this real intense fight about something one night. We were both crying a lot. And then Calley said that she thought the problem was commitment - we needed to put ourselves on the line. So I asked her and we just went to Las Vegas right away before either of us changed our minds."

Peter finished his drink. "I don't know what it is. I need her in this weird way. Right now, she makes me feel like everything is out of my control, like I'm just letting my life spin itself out."

We sat until nearly two when the bar closed. I offered dull advice. I tried to tell him that he had to distinguish between his own problems and Calley's. That he couldn't blame himself for hers. He never heard me; I was just filling in the pauses while he gathered his thoughts.

"Should I take you back to Charles'?" l asked when we stood outside the bar.

"No," he said flatly, looking at me and shaking his head.

I saw them together several times after that. Peter had taken a large studio for himself on Washington Boulevard near Western, just below

Koreatown. He was painting again, preparing for a show. Calley had been waiting up for him that night when he came home from the bar and they had talked until morning. They had determined to make something of their marriage. When I saw them at his studio, Calley seemed to be terribly happy. There was about Peter a certain aura of imminent success that I think attracted her, almost as if they were meeting for the first time. She talked excitedly about his paintings and she tried to involve him with her theater group, having him do the sets for their new play. But behind her enthusiasm, her lurking anger could be felt. She was too quick to take my side in any conversation, to talk to me about the books that Peter hadn't read. Her subtle jabs at my friend were becoming more and more obvious, and it seemed only a matter of time before the pressure would blow her wide open.

"I think she's fucking Charles," Peter told me one evening when Calley had stepped into the other room. "He was over the other night when I came home from the studio. Andrea is on the road right now. They acted a little weird." He looked toward the door where Calley had gone. "I guess it's my fault," he continued. "I sort of threw them together. I mean, Calley's always on me about being too possessive. She hates jealousy. I guess maybe I did leave them alone one or two times to show her I didn't care. But I really didn't think anything would happen."

In October, Peter had his show, at a gallery on La Cienega. Charles brought some of Andrea's friends and they bought a few of Peter's paintings for quite a lot a money. Calley beamed all evening, and it looked again as if she and Peter were really making a new start.

She was wearing the black dress that she had worn to the party the night they'd met. She looked absolutely incredible. It was as if her beauty alone were enough for her that evening. After the show, we went out for something to eat with the owner of the galery
and several critics, all of whom spent much of
their time fussing over Peter. Calley took the back seat gracefully, still happy to let Peter have his night.

After a few drinks, one of the critics invited us over to his place in Venice for a hot tub and some designer weed. I excused myself. Calley stood abruptly and asked me if I'd mind taking her home. She kissed Peter and said that she was tired, then she apologized to the others, making the prettiest exit imaginable.

She was quiet as we walked to the car and quiet as we got in. As I pulled away from the curb, she put her hand gently on my arm., "I know you don't like me at all." Her voice was quiet, resigned. I didn't answer, I was think-ing that you never could be sure with an actor, if anything was real. "He just shouldn't give me such a chance," she said. "It's too easy for me. It just makes a circle. If I'm horrible to him, I hate him for taking it. It's very important to me that you shouldn't hate me."

"Why?" I asked.

"Because you're Peter's friend and I don't want you to think any less of him." She let go of my arm and looked out the window. After while, I thought I heard her crying.

I dropped her off outside her apartment. She turned and looked closely at me. "You really mustn't hate me." She said and got out of the car.

I watched her until she was inside the door and then I drove away. As I turned the corner, a large black limousine was turning onto Havenhurst.

When Calley had looked at me, there had been no sign of tears in her eyes.

I woke up abruptly at four in the morning. Charles was pounding on my
door. His eyes were glassy and he was covered with sweat. "We've got to get
Peter," he said.
Something was obviously very wrong. I slipped into my clothes and we
started out. "Do you mind driving?" he asked. His voice was like a little
boy's, weak and helpless. "I think he's gone to his studio."
We took my car and I drove towards Western. Charles tapped nervously at
the dashboard, then he sat on his hands and immediately began to shuffl e
his feet. He was frightened.
"Andrea came back tonight," he said, looking at his knees. "l've been… well
I've been doing a thing with Calley. I don't think Peter knew. I was over
there tonight, just after you brought her home. Anyway, Andrea wasn't due
back for another two weeks, but there were some hassles with the booking
in Kansas City and she came back early. She never liked Calley. God, I wish
none of this had happened."
He was quiet for a moment and then continued, still looking at his knees,
"Andrea came over to Calley's. I guess she'd come home and, when I wasn't
there, she knew where to come. She had the Madsen…Jesus."
He started to vomit.

At the trial, Andrea Moon testifi ed that she was only sorry that she hadn't
gotten Charles as well. "His head was played by that chick. All of them,
that little bitch she was married to, Charlie, all of them. What the hell
did they think I'd do? They live in some kind of dream world or something;
and, honey, I've still got more money than all of them put together."
She pleaded temporary insanity and received a sentence of fi ve years at
the California Institute for Women at Chino. While the publicity increased
her sales enormously, the record company was still forced, for appearances
sake, to terminate her contract. Her poster was taken down from the Sunset
Strip.
Calley's funeral was small and quiet. The body was cremated as there was
hardly enough of it left to bury. Justin went to live with his grandmother,
so that life did not change much for him.
Peter was not at the funeral. He was at UCLA Medical Center recovering
from a total collapse. When Charles and I had reached his studio that
night, we'd found the door open. We went inside. Peter had taken off all of
his clothes and covered himself from head to foot with his paints. He was
running from one end of the room to the other, smashing himself into the
white walls of the studio, then rubbing against them in an orgasm of rage.
He turned towards us as we entered, and I could see the red of his blood
among the swirl of colors that covered him. "This is my world," he screamed
at us, pointing an accusing purple fi nger, "and every fucking bit of it
belongs to me."

LES BOHEM IS A MUSICIAN, POET AND SCREENWRITER FROM LOS ANGELES. AS A MUSICAN, HE WAS
A MEMBER OF SPARKS AND GLEAMING SPIRES HE RELEASED HIS ACCLAIMED SOLO ALBUM MOVED
TO DUARTE IN 2016. AS A SCREENWRITER HE HAS WRITTEN A NIGHTMARE ON ELM STREET 5: THE
DREAM CHILD, DAYLIGHT AND DANTE'S PEAK AMONG A NUMBER OF OTHERS. FIND OUT MORE
ABOUT HIM AT LESBOHEMSWONDERFULWORLDOFLESBOHEM.COM/ AND ORDER HIS NEW BOOK
OLD FRIENDS AT A PARTY AT PROLIFICPRESS.COM/BOOKSTORE/.

FRAGMENTED

SIRENS

PHOTOS
BY
JOHN
LEVY

I consider myself a motion picture maker. But still photography has been part of my life as long as motion. And more often than not they bleed into each other. I picked up still photography in my mid teens around the same time I began to experiment with film and video. Inspired across both formats by works from Ralph Steiner to Francesca Woodman and Gordon Parks. As a kid I'd leave my local movie house and take a photo walk home. When on set I take as many still as possible whether with my phone, Canonet or DSLR. Whether it's medium format, 35mm, video or screen captures from my videos, frozen or fleeting - I'm always making pictures. And I am grateful to have a place and people to share them with.

(Several images featuring the dancers in white dresses are screen captures, as well as photos, from my short film *The Disappearance* (2017))

- John David Levy

JOHN LEVY IS A NATIVE OF NOVATO, CA. AND COMES FROM A CREATIVE FAMILY. HIS MOTHER WAS AN ACTRESS AND PAINTER. HIS SISTER IS AN ART CURATOR. HIS BROTHERS ARE MUSICIANS AND BUILDERS. HIS NEPHEW A MUSIC PRODUCER.

HIS PASSION FOR CINEMA BEGAN IN EARLY CHILDHOOD AND HIS WORK AS A FILMMAKER BY HIS MID TEENS WORKING WITH VIDEO, 8MM AND 16MM CAMERAS AND EDITING ON FLAT BEDS AND AVID.

AFTER HIGH SCHOOL HE STUDIED FILM AT COLLEGE OF MARIN FWHILE VOLUNTEERING AS A PRODUCTION ASSISTANT ON NUMEROUS STUDENT FILM PRODUCTIONS FOR FRIENDS AT THE ACADEMY OF ART, SF.

IN 2009 HE TOURED ARTIST RESIDENCIES IN THE MEDITERRANEAN (SAINT EXUPERY, NICE, FRANCE. SIENNA, ITALY. BARCELONA, SAN SEBASTIAN, SPAIN). FINDING HIS VOICE AS A FILMMAKER.

IN 2010 HE CO-FOUNDED THE PRODUCTION COMPANY AND COLLECTIVE LA BELLE AURORE FILMS. AND DIRECTED THE PARALLEL LINES/RSA/PHILIPS COMPETITION SHORT, CODA.

IN 2011 HE DIRECTED THE EXPERIMENTAL LOVE STORY, THE GHOST OF LOVE.

IN 2012 HE DIRECTED THE AWARD WINNING SHORT FILM TABULA RASA. LATER THAT YEAR HE BEGAN PRE-PRODUCTION ON HIS FIRST FEATURE BASED ON THE AWARD WINNING SHORT.

IN 2013 HE DISBANDED FROM LBA FILMS AND PUT ALL HIS RESOURCES INTO CARING FULL TIME FOR HIS MOTHER AFTER BEING DIAGNOSED WITH VASCULAR DEMENTIA. STAYING INVOLVED IN NUMEROUS CAPACITIES WITH OTHER SHORT FORM PROJECTS AND THE INDEPENDENT FILM COMMUNITY.

AS OF 2016 HE IS IN A STATE OF RESET BOTH PERSONALLY AND CREATIVELY, BACK IN DEVELOPMENT OF SEVERAL FEATURES WHILE WORKING AS A FREELANCE VIDEOGRAPHER, EDITOR AND PHOTOGRAPHER. AND RETURNING TO SHORT FORM WITH, THE DISAPPEARANCE.

BIO FROM JOHNDAVIDLEVY.COM

SUBLIMINALS

by Robert Monell

If you go down in the woods today
You're sure of a big surprise
If you go down in the woods today
You'd better go in disguise!

--The Teddy Bear's Picnic.

"With nothing to stand as a barrier against the void,

Where there is neither horizon nor upright,

Nor surface,

Nor height [...]"

--Antonin Artaud

Prologue: 3000 BCE. On the outskirts of the city of Uruk, ancient
Iraq. A ziggurat in the Persian desert surmounted by a temple
consecrated to a nameless demon. Anisha, a woman of indeterminate
age with graying hair, dressed in a long white gown and wearing
a black veil over her face, is led into a room within the temple.
The room has reddish granite walls with screaming demon faces
sculpted into them. An inverted pentagram enclosed in a circle is
carved into the white marble fl oor. A priest swaddled in black
robes leads her into the center of the pentacle. She kneels and
lowers her head. In a corner of the room another priest slowly
bangs on a drum. A large man, also clad in black and wearing a
red bandana, is holding a large executioner's sword. He positions
himself in front of the only exit. No one must disturb the death
ritual.

--

Early 31st century CE. The Zero Vector: Anisha, a deep thinker as
her name indicates, squints, triggering her auto-telezoom function,
looking through the external skin of the shuttle as it passes
over ancient railway graveyards now covered in gray bio-contam-
inated dust. The shuttle is speeding over seemingly endless rows
of freight cars loaded with such 23rd century military equipment
as tanks, heavy artillery and troop carriers, the useless junk of
a previous century's war. At the very moment of breaking free of

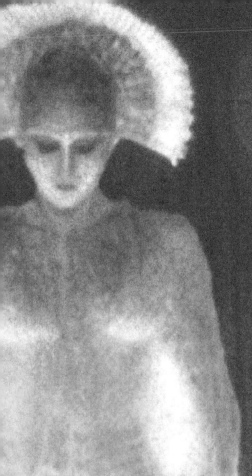

the artificial atmosphere of Earth-2 she is
drifting into thoughts of the demon Amy, who
in her mind has the appearance of a human
shaped mass of liquefied metal. She immediately dismisses the thoughts, not wanting to give
thought sanctuary to a demon. She hears distant thumping and crashing noises which have
an industrial quality to them. She is immersed
in thoughts and sounds she has carried in
her subconscious mind since she was a child.
Anisha is 30 years old, was born on the equa-
torial research center of New Africa, and has
superior psi skills. She is wearing a standard
Year Seven Space Systems silver shuttle suit.
It's not a good time, she whispers to herself.
Not a good time to feel the fear hardwired
into her consciousness. She was sure of that.
It always came and went without warning. It
had something to do with blood, the texture
of taste of blood. Sometimes she thought she
was under the curse of a lesser god or demon.
But then she recalled that she didn't believe
in the old gods and demons. So why was she
thinking about them?

She brushes away the thoughts, not needing to
be distracted. A beam shoots out from her eyes,
projecting a scene onto the cabin's wall from
F.W. Murnau's silent film NOSTERATU. A faded
black and white image of the rat-like vampire carrying a coffin. She tips her head back
allowing for psi enhanced listening as a Year
Seven Systems Class C A.I. narrates the presentation in measured tones and redirects her
attention to the image stream on her cubicle
wall, a feed of nonstop plasma, holograms, video, thought projection, photographs, Art from
the Old Earth, Earth-2 and Sphere generated
content, including all portals. She watches as
the stream settles into silent 3D black and
white images from a mid 20th century Eastern
European science fiction film. She is amused
by the thousand year old images as she listens to the presentation:

"SUBLIMINALS: A concept from Year Seven Systems: a game within an alternate reality. This
is not what used to be called Virtual Reality.
Subliminals is a game platform within the
Y7X3 Sphere, capable of supporting numerous
candidates. The Sphere contains numerous hidden portals into other dimensions. It contains
a multi-verse of potential realities. No equip-

ment is needed to play the game. Consider this a brief, friendly primer—

The Sphere is an artificial planet, 30 miles high, wide, and with a 30 mile circumference, constructed with a Saturn alloy developed by Year Seven Systems. The presence of dark matter and negative space within the sphere allows for space to be expanded beyond conventional parameters. There is no sidereal or linear time, nor is there only three dimensional space within the Sphere. To simplify temporal orientation the Accelerator, responsible for all event reporting within the Sphere, has set the year at 3024 CE. The temperature at all points, from the bottoms of oceans to the summits of mountains, is regulated at a mild 70 degrees Fahrenheit. The internal atmosphere is enhanced oxygen. There are oceans and mountain ranges inside because of the availability of flexible space. However, the Sphere also represents the Zero Dimension. Dynamic Heatmaps are psi-accessible for orientation..

The creation of the Sphere was post Big Pulse, the electromagnetic event which ended all wars, terrestrial communication and made all Earth energy grids inoperative. But that was the Old Earth. The Sphere is located in AU (Alternate Universe) Y7X3, an alternate dimension located and exclusively accessed by Year Seven Systems. It is not in outer space, in any independent solar system or the Earth's orbit, but one can access it from a platform where the Old Earth's moon existed before it was vaporized in the first Beta War. It exists in a bandwidth generated, expanded and re-engineered with D (Dark) energy, developed by Year Seven Systems and then boosted into code protected Triple Gain Strength. Here the Old Earth is an irrelevant factor as a planet which had been nearly uninhabitable after the great climate catastrophe and the Big Pulse. Most Upper life forms now inhabit Earth-2, a parallel dimension also located, developed and maintained by Year Seven Systems. The Thought Gain Control methodology holds sway on all media platforms, psychic fields, wavelengths and physical locations within the Sphere. To access the Sphere, though, once must power past the moon platform and achieve a physical location 500 miles above the atmosphere of Earth-2, which is an exact replica of the Old Earth and contains all its geographical, physical and human memory; or it can be accessed through a port achieved by Zero Vector transference.

This was all made possible by the discovery of the Quintessence/Scalar Field 0101A, accessible via a system fueled by D-Energy.. The Scalar Field was finally unlocked and its mysteries harnessed by Year Seven Systems in the late 22nd Century. It can power subliminals and all thought waves into multiple dimensions and can be directed into the consciousness of any living being. Nothing is real and everything is real in a D-Energy powered subliminal. These subliminals are not to be confused with the subliminal messages embedded in advertising messages, graphics, films and broadcasts of the 20th Century. The point is not to think, not to plan, not to imagine, not to resist. The subject must clear his or her mind and just accept, just be. One must be in what could be termed a Zen state to access the subliminals. The subject need not move, speak or react in any way. One must just be content to be within the Subliminal. They will gently, inexorably mold the subject's consciousness for brief or long time periods.

Once inside the Sphere, in the Tetragrammaton Reception Area, the Collators will beam subliminal scenes, images, messages and sounds into the subconscious mind of the participant. Subliminals can be activated by simply concentrating on the word Subliminal and deactivated by concentrating on the words End Subliminal.

But the subject must think of nothing else except the access and exit words. The concept is to activate and interact with as many subliminals as possible within a timeframe set by the Accelerator. Finding, entering and interacting within alternate reality portals will be awarded with bonus points. Once again, no physical movement is necessary. The subject will, though, have the experience of physical movement at times.

During a game all oral communication is banned except in Accelerator approved areas and monitored by Collators. Talking areas with be indicated by approved signage. The Accelerator sets the internal speed and mission of events while the Collators act as referees. The Collators, when they appear in three dimensional space-time, have the appearance of humanoid shadows captured on negative film. Sometimes they can appear as color coded (green, red, white, blue, magenta) human forms who will appear to referee certain situations. Along with oral communication the writing of any kind of text on any media is banned except on designated Collating devices.

Everyone is equipped with their own portable Vesica Piscis (VP), a fish shaped energy system modeled on the mystical Eye of Horus, which can be comfortably held in anyone's hand or worn in a holster. They are the next best tool to a physical implant. They are capable of transmitting and receiving numerous types of known and unknown energy. The eye of the fish is a both the transmitter and receiver of D energy. They can also be set on Laser and can be used to fire a death ray. A laser burst on this setting can be fatal at ranges up to one kilometer. There are certain concealed areas within the sphere which are embedded with an Eye of Horus portal, with which the VP can be recharged. Games are used for training, reeducation and entertainment. Remember, once you play the game you are never the same. Subliminals have the capacity to mold you into a completely new entity from the inside out. End of tutorial. Thank you for your participation."

Anisha removes her headset and immediately feels a low level anxiety about what she has heard.

[Subliminal: a series of Kabalistic symbols, Emblemas alquimicos, diagrarmas Ocultas y Memoria, the multi dimensional Tree of Life, and more, are entered into Anisha's subconscious by the Accelerator as one of the preparations for entering into the Sphere. It will be part of the Sub C databank available to her during the game.]

The landing bay for the shuttle leads directly into the Tetragrammaton Room, the gateway to the Sphere and the games within, including the numerous hidden dimensional portals. Embedded into the floor of the room is a sprawling septagram, capable of detaining, barring or trapping demons. As she looks down into the seven pointed star Anisha is besieged by more subliminals as she proceeds through the landing bay. In a decontamination grotto she is fitted by android greeters into a protective full diving skin which guards against all known forms of radiation, moisture, cold and is resistant to puncture by high speed objects. Somehow she knows her goal is to make it all the way to the Yesod Area, the Final Room, and to interact with her target.

Anisha stands in the middle of the septagram watching a holographic heat map display of a large man, about 30 years old. He has an intense, brooding look on his face. Target, written in red caps, flashes over his image. She stares into the eyes of the man, attempting to read something in them. The name Seth then replaces the word target, also in flashing red lettering. She is still thinking of the tutorial information and knows she can't depend on any help from outside of the Sphere. Suddenly, the thought of blood is overwhelming. She can taste it. The salty flavor fills her dry mouth, refreshing her. She clears her mind and turns her thoughts toward her mission, which seems vague and rather pointless. But that is negative thinking, something that is frowned on by the Accelerator.

****

Exterior. Mirror-cam view of Seth, at another point within the Globe, looking up at the words embedded on the façade of the Ministry of Behavior. "One must be radically shocked out of the banality and conformity of the reality before us. Then we can play the Game." It's a motto of the Accelerator, imprinted in gold lettering over all entrances and exits within the Sphere. However, there is only correct entrance and only one correct exit to each and every area. That fact makes the Accelerator's whims, moods, rules and regulations all the more intimidating to some. Seth has just completed his upgrade within the engineering module. He lowers his eyes to two words, rather crudely painted in black, underneath the Accelerator's motto: HUIS CLOS.

He immediately wonders if the words are some sort of code since they are in French. He knew what they meant, of course, he was first in languages at the Recovery Center in 3018. Or was it 3019? He can't remember exactly... And the motto was in text lettering. Was it an illegal or spurious text? Or, if deemed by the Accelerator, was it an exception to the rules? Or was it all an hallucination triggered by the Dystopian Consciousness Therapy course he had attended? Seth is a person who holds his high intelligence deep inside a silent hulk. He smiles, knowing the Game is on.

Seth's mode of dress is a popular one in certain gaming areas: a long, black brocade 19th century Empire Gentleman's Steampunk coat, worn over a white ruffled shirt, black pants and high black leather boots. He is topped off by a broad-brimmed, black leather, all-weather hat. He is, of course, subject to all Sphere generated imagery, waves and frequencies. Then he realizes if there is text or speech within the Sphere it was approved, monitored and analyzed by the Collators. Then a Subliminal surfaced, freezing him in place...

[Subliminal: Two children, male and female, sit transfixed in front of a large monitor. Computer generated images of small animated bears dancing in a wooded area flicker on the screen. The children are holding hands. Bright red flashes interrupt the images at regular intervals, which temporarily cause the children to stop smiling and assume a frown. The male is named Seth, the female is Anisha. There is an audio component, a low level recording of the The Teddy Bear's Picnic song.]

Seth often experienced this Subliminal as a distant memory which would suddenly come to mind. But who projected it into his subconscious mind? The Ministry? The Accelerator? Or was it a preparation for the game he was now playing?

An examination room in the Yellow Clinic. The drone camera tracks slowly across the top of the room looking down on the three bodies strapped to the examination tables. It's an XE mirror-cam which has no visible lenses and resembles a circular mirror with an approximately 12 inch circumference. Anisha slowly opens her eyes as the mirror-cam hovers over her. The silver, ovular drone hesitates, zooming in on her eyes which are now wide open. A medical drone bumps the XE aside

and opportunistically shoots an M (memory) ray into
her retina. Two female MDs enter, both young women who
appear to be twins, one of them squints into the light
emanating from the pad with which she examines the
eyes of the subject. Anisha looks up at the distant
face of the MD, it seems as if the face is an impossible
distance away. The twin MDs speak simultaneously to
Anisha, "Are you from the temple?" they ask repeatedly
until Anisha loses consciousness.

Anisha doesn't know who she is, where she is or how
she got there. She is simply there. She feels calm.
None of the long familiar background anxiety is on
the register. There is a sense of very low level pain
coming from somewhere in the back of her head. She
seems to recall a very sharp pain which was present
there a long time ago. She hears the MD's distant voice
speaking at very low volume. "You are Anisha, you are
in treatment." She hears the voice saying, "Non respon-
sive… we lost her." Then she seems to be looking down
at her dead body from the top of the room. She suddenly regains full consciousness. She didn't die. The
MDs were premature in their assessment. A male voice
breaks in at a higher volume, "No one needs to write,
text or think anything at all. The watching of all
unauthorized video input is also banned here. You may
listen to communications from the Accelerator or the
Collators. In some cases Collators or a Moderator may
allow writing, verbal communication and the watching
of plasma under strict supervision."

She doesn't really hear the communication. But it reso-
nates deep within… "All procreation driven and recreational sexual relations between any and all human

individuals is banned…. Recreational sex between humans and select android, robot, cyborg, artificial intelligence, and holographic forms are permitted when scheduled in view of Collating personnel."

The twin MDs chime in together. "You have artistic tendencies and are of no use to us, you can only destroy. We will work that out in therapy, or possibly within game action."

Anisha now realizes that she has already entered the Sphere and is actually in the Tetragrammaton Room, where initiates are examined and programmed. The clinical experience was just a programmed detour.   Just as she consciously accepts this she is projected to the Café Kabul, a designated oral communication area, where the Director hands her an illegal script. The Café is located in a dark, dirty underground area with very low lighting. It's actually a cavern formed by 21th Century petroleum engineers and later developed into a grimy, downscale Accelerator approved Mall.

The Director is a tall, thin man, dressed in a long black robe, with a heavy black beard. Anisha notices he is wearing a six pointed star necklace, the seal of Solomon. She is thinking of blood again. He smiles and doesn't say a word as she sits at the table compulsively reading the script:

Interior. Hallway. Night: Forward Tracking Shot slowing moving down the hallway. Smoke and pulsating green light fills the corridor. Seth's hand reaches out

toward a door which suddenly seems to open by
itself.

Interior. Strange Room. Night: The camera tracks
slowly forward through the room's window. The
room is dark and only the shape of a woman can
be seen. The room is suddenly fl ooded with light
as Seth enters and sees the Model, a woman of
about 25, tall, thin, with long red hair. She wears
a long white dress which clings tightly to her
body. A straight razor suddenly appears in Seth's
hand. He looks toward the Model whose dress is
now fl ushed with bright crimson splotches; the
anticipation of blood. Seth walks past her, drop-
ping the razor. He walks into a large, upright
oval mirror in the corner of the room. Inside the
mirror there is the sound of a strong wind and
thunder in the distance. Those sounds are over-
whelmed by loud, clashing electric guitar chords.
The music gradually increases in volume until
Seth has to hold his hands over his ears in an
attempt to block out the sound. He is fl oating
in a strobe-lit void.
Anisha looks up from the script.

"This is banned, you know. Reading a text, written
on unauthorized medium... paper! This is not the
20th century! "

The Director smiles, " Not really, it's an approved
area. There is no legal system in this dimension
in any case. If I am in error I will simply be
eliminated or frozen."

Anisha looks down, her default pose, "I have some
anxiety now."

" That will pass....and you will enter the Quintes-
sence" the Director reassures her as....

A silver skinned Collator quickly approaches.
The Director rises and moves back from Anisha.

The Collator (taking a hose from a compartment
in his chest and pointing the nozzle at the Director), fl res a stream of chemical ice. The job of
a Collator is to not only collect and combine but
to remove all disruptive elements. The Director
hears the words Banned Action Verifi ed in his
mind just as the stream instantaneously freezes
him in place.

Anisha wonders if she is experiencing a Subliminal as maintenance units remove the frozen
Director. The maintenance team has removed the

script from her grip but now she "sees" the scenes described in the text, as if in a plasma. Film does not exist as it did in the 19th, 20th and 21st centuries. Everything is now on Plasma K Element, an invisible "cloud" where one can store data, graphics, video and access it through a personal Vesica Piscis.

Anisha is projected onto a back alley in Dura Europa. With some trepidation she enters the Vampire's Dream lounge. She notes there is an escape portal leading back to the Mall area. As she seats herself on a black leather recliner she notices the huge image of Bela Lugosi walking down a castle stairway in the film DRACULA, which is being shown on the wall sized plasma screen. A bright orange android waiter bends to whisper in her ear, "The game is everything. And in your game blood will be everything. Remember, "Blood is Life!."

A scene invades Anisha's consciousness. She watches it unfold with intense interest. It is the third millennium BCE.. Anisha watches herself as she walks through the streets of Uruk, covered with a black chador, tracking a scantily clad young man. He is staggering from one side of the narrow alleyway to the other. He is either ill or intoxicated. He rushes up to the man, drags him to the ground and knells over him, placing her mouth on his neck. She suddenly looks up, her mouth dripping with blood. Fade to Red.

At another point in Dura Europa a tunnel surveillance cam tracks Seth as he wanders toward a blue light which emanates from what seems the end of the tunnel. He hears a voice guiding him, "It's directly ahead, keep going. Someone you know is at the end of the line."Seth holds his three pronged torch up when he sees a figure in a dark corner. Suddenly, a Collator appears, dressed in all white medical garments. The three prongs of the flame also have a Kabalistic significance which Seth considers as a form of protection. The Collator sends a thought message, "You must come with me. I have to take you to a clinic for emergency surgery." The Collator suddenly produces a syringe-like surgical probe which he inserts into Seth's chest. Seth has an immediate narcotic vision of the Collator, who in the hallucination is wearing a white martial arts gi and a red headband. He suddenly produces a small green mid 20th Century style pistol, aims at the plasma camera broadcasting the scene, and fires. Fade to Red.

[Subliminal: Anisha is being driven to an unknown site. She squints into the bright, multi-colored lights of the approaching traffic on the freeway. It is unclear to her whether she is in a ground vehicle or an aircraft in a holding pattern allowing for incoming flights. Red, white, green blinking lights and whooshing noises suggest air traffic. She blinks and is suddenly back at the clinic as the Subliminal continues. Or is she? She is dragged into a room by a large woman wearing a white medical smock. "It is a drug!" she hears the woman's metallic voice telling her. But, of course, it's all in her mind, her subconscious, and she will remember nothing whatsoever. She somehow knew she had an immediate assignment to move into a cubicle beyond where she was located. The large woman is now wearing a headset which looks wet and bleeds red fluid. "She can hear my blood," Anisha thinks aloud. This is immediately followed by a rapidly edited series of images of ancient looking men with long beards, close ups of ants, scorpions and other aggressive insects fighting amongst themselves, deep sea creatures without eyes, green tinted volcanic magma, and thousands of other images. It all seems to be visible in the same micro-second. Cut to an image of what appears to be a human sized, carrot shaped creature with slits for eyes. It has a stream of green fluid dripping from its mouth. It is sitting at a con

panel and moving a skeletal hand over
a group of small orbs which glow a soft
pink. She has the sense of being in an
unknown fl ying vehicle. She begins to
slowly proceed, as if being drawn by a
powerful magnet, though a lemon colored rectangle and is fi nally deposited
in a room fi lled with female sex robots,
the oldest models, clad only in black
see-through negligees and stockings.
They all wear sunglasses and black
leather gloves. She sees herself tied
to a medical examination table. A long
needle held by a stainless steel hand
injects her in the temple with a clear
fl uid. The thought of blood overwhelms
her. She can taste it again. She is at
the Zero Dimension.

This is wiped from her consciousness,
replaced by an image of Seth walking
through a damp, dark tunnel in the Dura
Europa Underworld. He is holding the
three pronged torch to light his way as
he hurriedly makes his way toward the
Reactivation Room.] The subliminal is
over. She will have no conscious memory
of it whatsoever as she shakes herself
into full consciousness.

Seth once said his real father was the false prophet Nostradamus. Maybe his real father, their real father, was some kind of demon. Seth is seized with the realization that his father was the patron Lord of the city of Canaan and that the Nostradamus name was a sham. Seth would ask for the gift of fire when the time was right. A streaming scene of Seth, watching a video about ancient Egypt in which the main character is an aged Pharaoh, flashes through her mind. She sees the scene play out a in five sided mirror: the Pharaoh, in full regalia, quickly rises from his throne in the pyramid, he walks up to wall decorated with images of Osiris. He waves his hand and a hidden door swings open. He is removing his garments as he walks down a dark hallway. He stops at the end of the hallway in from of a tall chamber door with a circular handle made of solid gold. Very slowly and with considerable effort, since there is heavy resistance, ye pulls the door open by the handle, Bright red light floods out of the room, which he enters, closing the door behind him. He staggers and falls to the floor, writhing in pain. He slowly transforms into a wolf man, complete with large fangs and a long snout. Foam drips from his mouth. The red light of the room is blinding, but he stands and makes his way toward a figure chained to a wall. The figure is revealed, when he draws near, to actually be his human self, before the transformation. He tips the head of his chained double to one side and bites into the neck, drawing and drinking in a flow of fresh blood.

Anisha is back at the Tetragrammaton Room and she's thinking about blood, human blood, its texture and taste. She wonders if she ever really left the room. She craves daylight, which seems a million miles away. She imagines herself as a bat floating just under the ceiling of a dark, damp cave. Then she freezes up and is short of breath as she becomes aware of the Mudman in the corner of the room. The Mudman is well over seven feet tall and covered from head to foot with slimy brown mud. A foul odor fills the room. Some kind of banned oral communication is transmitted by the Mudman. It sounds like he's struggling to say the word Love, but she's not sure since it's anything but clearly articulated. Nonetheless she answers, "But I can't love or accept love…. I just don't trust!" She blinks several times in quick succession after which the Mudman disappears.

The teeming city of Dura-Europa is at the core of the Sphere It has become obvious to Seth that he is a player in the game within the Game. He knew he would be player, like it or not, and that Anisha would also be a player. And that it wouldn't end well….

He didn't want to play a role in an illegal production but felt he was being compelled to act it out. The production was now and he had no idea what It meant or who wrote it. The previous scenes also didn't make sense to him. Were they Subliminals or something else? He plays them back in his mind:

[1]A silver colored room, long and narrow. It is equipped with a series of walls, each about 2 meters high. The walls run from one side to the other of the room, so one cannot walk around them. The walls are spaced 3 meters apart down the length of the corridor, which at first glance seems to stretch to infinity. The walls are painted a glossy silver and if one looks closely it is possible to see your reflection in the silver paint. Seth is seated in a metal chair directly in front of the first wall, into which he is staring intently. A male voice murmurs in his mind. "It starts whenever you want," it whispers to him. A whooshing noise is heard and a hand appears holding a Vesica Picis, pointing it at Seth's head. A brief, sharp shriek is heard. Then silence. "You will see her when arrive at the ninth wall"

[2] Seth suddenly finds himself beyond the second wall. "I crashed through," he thought, since his entire body ached as if he had run into a hard barrier. A small remote plasma camera floats up to his face. A tiny red light blinks rapidly into his eyes. A voice which speaks to him from deep in his mind says "I am here to guide you through this room." An attractive young woman in a silver leather outfit, which seems to have been made with the same material as the walls, suddenly appears behind the camera, which she grabs and holds up to her eyes. "I am here to prepare you for the furnace room" she says in a voice which he vaguely remembers hearing some nights just before sleep.

[3] The Furnace Room, beyond the third wall, is a small space within curved metal walls. At an entrance beyond the third wall. Seth takes a step forward. The small space expands into a large area with a metal floor on which burnt human bodies are arranged in circular patterns. This room is very cold but shows signs of great heat on the scorched walls and low ceiling].

Seth suddenly realizes that he has been transmitted here with only a brief warning. There is no training here and none will come. Seth then realizes he's been in the game module all along and that it was time for yet another Subliminal:

 [The Subliminal presents itself as scenes in a film script illustrating events in the late 20th Century.

Scene X: Interior. Seth's Apartment. Night

The camera watches through his apartment window as Seth is finishing building a model of a gothic cathedral which is set up in the middle of the room. He stands back, studying the model. Grabbing a tin of lighter fluid from a shelf he quickly drenches the model with it. He slowly smiles. He takes a lighter out of his pocket and holds it close to the model but not close enough to ignite the fluid.

Seth: "Forgive them father, for they know not what they do...."

Fade to Black on image of model cathedral.

Scene Y: Exterior. A huge stadium. Night. Seth is among the crowd watching a Black Metal concert, the group's name, BANDE Z, flashes on a towering fluorescent display overhead.. A tall, black man wearing an exotic Macumba headdress approaches him. Seth slightly nods in his direction. Close up of black man handing off a tiny voodoo doll to Seth

Scene Z. Seth's apartment. Night A drone camera watches outside the Seth's apartment window as he sits at a table holding a large butcher knife in one hand, the voodoo doll in the other. He places the doll on a cutting board and holds the knife over its neck. A video playback of the concert appears on his wall. A fast tracking shot around Hister, the drummer, who is dressed in blue workman's clothes and has a Mohawk haircut. Close up of the voodoo doll which is now dressed in the same clothes and has a Mohawk haircut. Seth suddenly arises, places the doll in a glass jar, and ignites the doll with a low level beam from his Vesica Picis Plasma image of Hister suddenly bursting into flames.]

Events within the Sphere: Anisha looks up and stares for an extended period at overhead light projections. The she realizes that she is in the final phase. She

is now climbing a narrow ladder toward a thought module built into the wall of the Sphere. When she reaches it she yanks the hatch open and pulls herself in, seating herself on a comfortable leather couch. She finds a headset hanging overhead and puts it on. The scene unfolds as if in a 20th Century film: A stone walled basement with a wooden cross at its center. A group of cultists, dressed in long red gowns with black pointed hoods over their heads emerge from the shadows leading a middle aged woman, wearing what looks like an old burlap sack over her. She has frizzy gray hair and a drugged stare. The woman is tied to the cross by the cultists. Their movements and the entire scene proceed with what seems an excruciating slowness, as if a religious ritual acted out in very slow motion. Anisha imagines that she walks over the bound woman, tips her head aside and bites into her neck. The taste of blood fills her mouth. Close Up of Seth, a small silver crucifix, complete with Christ on the cross, hangs upside down from his ear. His eyes narrow and a sharp point of crimson light burns in their center.

A cultist, a very old, gaunt priest with long gray hair, with glazed over eyes speaks.

Cultist: "We of the unholy Inquisition due hereby sanction you…"

The cultist ties a noose around the neck of the woman and pulls it tight until her head drops to one side after some choking. Suddenly, Seth arises from a seat, the lights go up and we see he is among an audience made up of some young people with violently colored hairstyles, a few street people types and several scantily clad women who look like models.

Seth (pulling a glass flask of whiskey from inside his coat): "Ha! I drink to you… fucking hypocrites! I drink to your death!" Seth then rushes over to a young, attractive female member of the audience pulls her out of her seat trying to force her to kneel down. A muscular young man attempts to intervene but Seth smashes the glass flask onto his face. The man screams holding his now blood smeared face in his hands, falling to his knees, screaming. Seth quickly pulls out of his jacket a small object which looks like a cigarette lighter. He points it at the young woman who is backing away in horror. A jet of flame shoots out at the woman, setting her head ablaze. She screams in pain and horror. Fade to Black.

Voices (in unison): "Out! Out! Out! Throw the bastard out! Out! Out! Out! Throw the bastard out! Outl Out! Out! Throw the bastard out!"

The voices continue in unison over black until the words became an very loud and continued chanting. The chanting fades into the rising sound of what sounds like military marching. The sound of leather boots hitting pavement rises and gradually fades. Flash image of the icon of the Sacred Heart of Jesus as a loud male voice screams incoherently.

Anisha removes the headset and hears the voice of the module, "End of Game--Time Warning… End of Game--Time Warning…."

The tunnel still recedes before him but Seth senses he has reached his intended destination. He climbs a ladder to a surface portal. Something was bursting into his imagination, and it wasn't a replayed Subliminal. He felt like a creative partner in the game now. He surfaces into a deserted back street. Seth stands frozen in a dark square next to a looming Gothic Cathedral. He stares up at the moon which illuminates his face. Suddenly a shadow passes over him. Long Shot of the moon with clouds passing over it.

He is suddenly bathed in an aquamarine light. He reads aloud the words of an oath which scroll across the surface of the midnight moon, as if it were an occult poem projected by a cosmic power.

" I swear to Master Satan that this Cathedral will burn.
It will illuminate the night with righteous fl ames,
It will burn their minds, their bodies, their white souls,
They will scream for salvation but they will be frozen in place.

And then the city will burn and its fl aming vermin will fl ee.
My screams will pursue them into the night.
But there will be no escape,
There will be no escape from the inferno..."

Seth enters a small graveyard cordoned off by a heavy metal fence behind the Cathedral. Aquamarine light coming from above illuminates the graves as he studies the names on the stones. Close Up of a stone engraved with: Father N. V. Mier 1900-1980 RIP. Seth points his Vesica Piscis device at the gravestone. The device emits a high pitched sound and a thin ray of magenta light. The gravestone moves back a few feet, revealing an opening in the ground. He quickly enters the opening... Seth climbs down a metal ladder back into the seemingly endless tunnel, which is illuminated with sickly yellow light. The sounds of dripping water and scurrying rodents break through the silence. He reaches the fl oor of the tunnel. He walks through the tunnel for some distance, his boots splashing into shallow puddles of stagnant, septic water.

He stops suddenly at the edge of a deep pool of water in a darkened area. He points the device out over the water, illuminating it. A wooden raft is fl oating several meters into the pool. He presses several buttons on the device which emits a humming sound, pointing it toward the raft. The raft moves closer and the body of a naked woman which has been tied down is revealed. The woman's corpse is devoid of color and has slash wounds on the wrists, ankles, throat and side. The raft is now at the edge of the pool, close enough for Seth to pull toward him. He walks over the edge of the tunnel where several buckets are sitting. He produces a white surgical mask from inside his cape, pulls it over his nose and mouth and then picks one of the buckets up, carries it over to the raft and pours the bright green liquid contents onto the corpse. A sizzling sound is heard. He watches as the thick green fl uid gradually dissolves the corpse, leaving only a partial skeleton. He suddenly screams. The scream is loud and long. Seth then kicks the raft out into the pool again. Seth watches the raft move away into darkness. A rush of loud, harsh electronica is heard as the scene shifts.

Seth is now on a back street in Dura-Europa. A large glowing sign looms over him: YESOD AREA. He's not sure if he's acting out a Subliminal or not. The uncertain feeling generates an anxiety wave in him as he moves down a narrow hotel corridor. The walls of the corridor are lined with pink wall paper embossed with impressionist style illustrations of fl oating fl owers. All the doors to the rooms have been left open and he beholds a different horrifi c scene in each one: a pile of decapitated human bodies, a pile of human heads in the next room, a huge rat, three feet tall and six feet long in another. An image of him being pounced on by the rodent and having his head bitten off fl ashes into his mind. Anisha's hand suddenly reaches out and pulls him into a plush lavender room.

Seth falls toward her. She forces him into a corner, suddenly biting into his neck. The taste of blood overwhelms her.

Endgame in the Yesod Area: Anisha is backing away from the Mudman, who has suddenly appeared just as she pulled Seth into the room. Her Sub C cam implant zooms in on the Mudman, who envelops her while ripping her leather suit off. She is on the fl oor covered with the squishy brown and black mass. She hears distant chanting male voices and has the sensation of being violated. And then see looks around her and at fl oor level sees many lit candles, as if placed there for an unknown rite. She lashes out and knocks several candles over. A fi re erupts in the room, rapidly engulfi ng her and the Mudman . She feels her skin being seared. Then she is freed from being under the slushy weight and the Mudman appears to have moved away. Seth, standing over her, feels the time has come to invoke his demon. He moans slowly and with volume. He then whispers "fire" and holds his open hand out as if to grasp an eternal flame. Anisha locates her suit and firmly grasps her Vesica Piscis, swinging it around to aim at the tall black figure approaching her. Seth reaches out to help her up as she fires an incinerating ray at him, instantaneously reducing him to a pile of gray ash. The flames subside, leaving only the ashes of Seth and the Mudman.

Anisha plays back the Endgame in her mind as she departs the Sphere in the Year Seven Systems shuttle. She had played the game by just being there. No thought or movement was required. The shuttle is now free of the electromagnetic shield which surrounds the Sphere. She powers on her memory playback, projecting it onto the cubicle wall. She sees the image of a gray pile of ashes in the Final Room. She thinks about Seth. He was once her brother. She had been aware that he had experienced human death but was rebuilt and reanimated as a Year Seven Class B cyborg. Considering herself, she knew she wasn't a hologram, a cyborg, an A.I., a perfect robot or a sex android. She knew she was human and real. She suddenly is overcome by a wave of anxiety, as if she were an insect floating on a wave in a turbulent ocean of space-time. A wave about to crash on a distant granite shore. She is one second away from obliteration. But that second has somehow been frozen and the ocean is now calm. She was about five minutes away from the docking bay on Earth-2.

She thought back to the Final Room incident. As Seth was disintegrating she thought she picked up a psi signal, perhaps it was a botched attempt at transmitting a Subliminal. She heard his voice, slowed down as in a digital code, tape or ancient vinyl recording playing at the wrong speed. It was saying over and over, in an insistent whisper "Remember to die…. Remember to die … ." At a lower level she also could also hear The Teddy Bear's Picnic song. She was breathing heavily and felt a distant sadness. The song always brought tears to her eyes.

The Zero Vector: As the shuttle approaches the Earth-2 protective shield Anisha hears a voice speaking to her. She immediately wonders if it is something generated in a Dark-Energy Area? She isn't sure where it comes from, but it seems like a reassuring inner voice whispering the name of the demon who presided over the multi-verse games. She also somehow knew not to say the name aloud. "Never speak the name of a demon," she said out loud, as if affirming herself. She instantly wiped the name from her consciousness.. Something assured her that she would never she see the face of the demon. It would remain faceless and unnameable in her subconscious. That's the way she wanted it to be. If she couldn't deny it, she could delete it. She had already forgotten Seth, deleted him forever.
Then the thought came all at once: Evil does not stop and take a break, nor does it take into consideration the suffering of its victims. It does what it does because it can. It is unstoppable, unnameable. If there is a blockage in its path it alters its course and continues around the obstruction. Most people don't understand the true nature of evil until it's too late. It's liquid, always hungry and always on the move. It usually has a face. To look into its face is painful, takes courage and is exhausting. And the evil knows that. The most powerful tool evil has in its arsenal is its ability to get good, highly intelligent people to underestimate it, to think "It'll just go away." That gives it space to grow and further embed itself in legitimate systems which it will corrupt from within.
She was on the verge of talking aloud as the thoughts continued. But was any of it evil?   Was it an ancient illness with which she had been infected? Or was it something inherited from a primeval ancestor? As those thoughts subside Anisha looks intently into the bottomless black of space in which she is immersed, trying to see beyond the gravitational lensing,, searching for something .

Epilogue: 3000 BCE.. Outskirts of Uruk, ancient Iraq. A ziggurat in the Persian desert. In the temple room the executioner's sword drips with fresh, scarlet blood. The priest places Anisha's severed head in a sack and carefully covers her headless body with a golden sheet. He nods in approval, slightly smiling.. He whispers to the executioner, "The remains shall be burned on the desert fl oor at midnight. She violated the code of the Nameless, she drank human blood . She died praying for death. That is a good thing. She has escaped from the pure negativity of countless lifetimes. She has escaped from evil."

A CELEBRATED WRITER AND FILMMAKER,
ROBERT MONELL IS ONE OF THE LEADING
AUTHORITIES ON EUROPEAN GENRE CINEMA IN THE WORLD.
HIS WORK HAS APPEARED IN A VARIETY OF ACCLAIMED BOOKS,
JOURNALS, MAGAZINES AND WEBSITES INCLUDING THE LANDMARK BLOG
HE CREATED, I'M IN A JESS FRANCO STATE OF MIND. HE IS ALSO AN
ADMINSTRATOR AT THE POPULAR FILM FORUM CINEMADROME.
FOLLOW HIM AT WWW.INSTAGRAM.COM/ROBERTMONELL/

The font I used for Robert's story is called Traveling Typewriter.
It is font made by Carl Krull from an old Danish
"Olympia Traveler de luxe" typewriter
made in western Germany.
Any inconsistencies found in its lettering and spacing
are deliberate and part of its charm.

FILM STILLS:
METROPOLIS, NOSFERATU, DRACULA, TRANS EUROPE EXPRESS, EDEN AND AFTER.

"The Bells isn't merely Lou Reed's best solo LP, it's great art.

Lou Reed is walking naked for once, in a way that invites comparison with people like Charles Mingus, the Van Morrison of "T.B. Sheets" and Astral Weeks, and the Rolling Stones of Exile on Main Street. The Bells is by turns exhilarating ("Disco Mystic," an exercise in churning R&B that should be a hit single, if there's any justice), almost unbearably poignant (all of the lyrics) and as vertiginous as a slow, dark whirlpool (the title opus).

There's a real band on this record, and these musicians are giving us the only true jazz-rock fusion anybody's come up with since Miles Davis' On the Corner period. And all through the LP, Reed plays the best guitar anyone's heard from him in ages.

With "The Bells," more than in "Street Hassle," perhaps even more than in his work with the Velvet Underground, Lou Reed achieves his oft-stated ambition — to become a great writer, in the literary sense.

You gave us reason to think there might still be meaning to be found in this world beyond all the nihilism, and thereby spawned and kept alive a whole generation whose original parents may or may not have been worthy of them. If one is to be haunted by ghosts, who's to say they're not specters of love pouring back from dead angels and living children?"

-Lester Bangs, Rolling Stone-

No Cure Needed:

An Interview With Craig Bell

by Jeremy R Richey

Hey Craig. Thanks so much for taking the time to participate in this Q&A about your remarkable career. I wanted to start off with a bit about your childhood if you don't mind. What was life like in Elmira, New York in the fifties and how old were you when your family relocated to Ohio?

I do not have any memories of my infancy in Elmira. My elder brother and I were born there but we moved shortly after my birth to Bath, NY and then to Buffalo when I was around two. I remember living in an apartment building there until my sister was born shortly after that and we moved to a home in Cheektawoga, a Buffalo suburb.

My father worked for the Lackawanna Railroad and as he moved up in the company we were on the move, next to Denville, New Jersey in 1959, where my other sister arrived. We lived there until 1961 when my dad was assigned to the railroad's headquarters in Cleveland, Ohio.

LACKAWANNA RAILROAD — *The Shortest Route between New York – Scranton – Binghamton – Elmira – Buffalo*

What type of music did your parents have in the house when you were a child and was there anything in particular that sparked your initial interest in music?

My folks were not big music fans, my mom liked Frank Sinatra and I remember hearing his records played on the family stereo, as well as LPs by Jackie Gleason and other big band leaders. My dad liked bagpipe music and had a few albums of that.

At an early age I became infatuated with the radio and listened whenever I could. I had a radio in the room I shared with my brother and would have it on constantly. I would listen to anything that I could find all over the dial. My love for auto racing came about when I sat on our neighbors' patio during a Memorial Day pool party in Cheektawoga in 1957, listening to the entire Indianapolis 500 race on the radio. Sam Hanks was the winner. As I grew older, I would keep a log of the stations I could bring in on my little table radio. My brother and I strung a bunch of wire across the rafters of our home's attic in Lakewood, Ohio so we would have greater reception. At night, I would listen to distant static-laden broadcasts, trying to hear the call letters and location of the stations. The furthest west I was able to hear was Denver. I could bring in signals from all over the east coast and deep south as well as the Midwest and Texas with ease. I heard all sorts of things, music, news, sports. A lasting memory was from 1968 when I fell asleep listening to a baseball game broadcast from the west coast. I awoke in the middle of the night to the reports of Robert Kennedy being shot in Los Angeles; at first I thought it was a dream of JFK's assassination, then realized it was all too real.

You would have been a teenager in the sixties when the British Invasion landed. Did any of those bands inspire you as you came of age? Also, even though you were a bit young when the initial rock n roll explosion hit were you a fan of artists like Elvis and the other Sun Records revolutionaries?

By this time, my radio fascination was in full swing so I was very aware of Elvis, Chuck Berry, Little Richard and other early rock and roll artists, as well as all the other pop artists that were wiped away by the arrival of The Beatles and other English bands, as well as the American acts who were having hits at the time like The Ventures and The Beach Boys. I also listened to the local Cleveland RnB stations as well as the big country station out of Akron, OH.

CKLW, a radio station out of Windsor, Ontario Canada was a powerful influence over all the Great Lakes region as to well me in Cleveland. Being across the river from Detroit, they played all the great sounds coming out of Tamla/Motown and more rock sounds on the charts and, being Canadian, they had a lot of the latest offerings from England first so there was lots of music to grab you.

Jumping ahead in time a bit, had you ever seriously thought about being in a band before you were approached by a few friends to form the legendary Mirrors?

On a Saturday afternoon in the summer of 1965, my friend Dave Davis and I spent an entire afternoon at the Beachcliff Theatre watching the Gerry and the Pacemakers movie, *Ferry Cross The Mersey*, multiple times. On the walk home we both decided we wanted to be in a rock and roll band. It was the only way to go! My only problem was my father would not allow me to own a guitar. He had previously said if I was going to play an instrument, it had to be a "real" one. I took lessons on the Trombone, which I learned to hate, and then switched to clarinet. I didn't care for that much either and never became very proficient on it. Since I couldn't own a guitar while still at home I did what I could to be near friends who did. I would help move their gear and hang around while they practiced. When I graduated high school I immediately moved out of my parents' house and, although still not able to play anything, started to look to join a band. After a 6 month stint in California in '70-71, I returned to Cleveland and ran into the fiancée of a school friend, Jim Crook, guitarist in Mirrors, at the Velvet Underground show (without Lou Reed) at the Agora. He had just returned from Army Service in Vietnam and told me he and his friend Jamie Klimek were planning to start a band. He invited me over to his place to hang out and listen to records after I told him I had recently purchased both the Syd Barrett solo LPs. After this meeting, and being around them for a while, they decided I qualified as the new bass player. Jamie handed me his bass guitar, showed me what note each string was tuned to and told me to figure out the rest for myself. I was in!!!

I've read in an older interview you gave that Mirrors, from the get go, didn't sound like anything else in the Cleveland area in the early seventies. Were you all aware of that at the time and would any of you have guessed just how influential and important the band would become?

We wanted to be successful from the start. I can't speak for anyone else in the band at that time, but I wanted to be a star and run around being chased by photographers and girls! I wanted to skeet shoot my gold records like my bass idol John Entwistle! Of course, I would have settled just for the chance to record, perform and tour. When the opportunity to start down that road came with the offer from Jamie, Jim I jumped at it. I especially liked the songs they had played for me that they were starting to write. They sounded like the bands I loved so much, English bands like The Kinks, The Who, The Troggs, Hawkwind and Roxy Music, along with American bands like Creedence, The Turtles, The Stooges, MC5, and The Velvet Underground.

How important was Lou Reed and The Velvet Underground to the sound that eventually became known as punk and modern rock in general?

It is pretty obvious now what a transcending influence Lou's songs and persona, along with the rest of VU, have been in the music that has come along since the early 1970's, when we first got together as Mirrors; but at that time he was still on the fringes of acknowledgment and appreciation by the mainstream music industry. We were true believers, then and now. His style was the bedrock from which we created our sound. There were many more influences from the four of us, but it all rose from a VU foundation.

Left to Right   JAIME KLIMEK   PAUL MAROTTA   CRAIG BELL   JIM CROOK   MICHAEL WELDON   JIM JONES

How did the pseudonym 'Darwin Layne' come about and how did playing with Rocket From The Tombs differ from your time with Mirrors?

I was fooling around with stage names and came up with that one while in Mirrors. No one else in the band used a stage name so I never took it too seriously. It was all part of the fun. When I joined RFTT, and had characters like Cheetah Chrome, Johnny Blitz, and Crocus Behemoth, I started to use Darwin. I was approached to join RFTT in the fall of 1974. Peter Laughner came to visit me at a house that Jamie and I shared. He asked if I would be interested in this new band he was putting together with David. Mirrors had been stagnant for a few months, no shows and hardly ever rehearsing, even though we had a space in the basement of the house. So I told Jamie I was going to check this thing out but still wanted to put Mirrors first, and if there were any conflicts, Mirrors would be my priority. This scenario happened at RFTT's first show with the new configuration in December at Extermination Night at the Viking Saloon where RFTT, Mirrors, and electric eels shared the bill. I didn't perform with Rocket, only Mirrors. By the time the second shared gig rolled around a couple of weeks later, I had been fired from Mirrors and was with RFTT full time. Considering how these days if you aren't in at least 3 bands, you aren't really trying. Those truly were different times.

I've been a bit obsessed with Peter Laughner ever since I first read about him as a teenager. His

personal demons aside, how do you view him and his work now more than forty years after his death?

I love and miss Peter very much. He passed so young yet left so many great recordings, many still needing a wider distribution. Peter was a friend and a fan. I was in awe of his musical and writing ability. I learned a lot in my short few years of being close to him.

You co-wrote one of the greatest songs of all time with Peter and what would become the core of Pere Ubu. Can you tell us a bit about how the brilliant "Final Solution" came about and what was the process of writing it like? Also what were your thoughts on the Pere Ubu version and also the Peter Murphy cover in the mid-eighties?

I was at our rehearsal space when David arrived and said he had a new song. He sat down and started banging out a beat on the side of an amp as he recited the words. I started playing along and when he came to the end of a line he said, "do something here". So I made noise, then went back to the beat for the next line, making a different noise at the end of that one. Third time around I did a climb back to the first note and banged away at the E while David shouted "I DON'T NEED A CURE!! I NEED A FINAL SOLUTION!" We had that worked out by the time the rest of the band arrived, after playing what we had, Peter added the B/E riff at the end, Cheetah kicked in some crazy lead work to go along with Peter's and Blitz knocked it out of the park. We knew we had a winner.

I was very pleased to see Pere Ubu record the song for their second single. There was a modification to the verse line but the rest played as RFTT conceived it.
In 1986, I was at my coke dealer Blase's house playing cribbage with MTV on in the background when I heard this familiar bass line. When they broke into the song I was floored. It was Peter Murphy covering "Final Solution." Blase didn't believe me when I told him I co-wrote that song!
Living the life, man!

You were involved in the creation of so many great songs that helped shape American Punk and Post-Punk in the seventies. Are there any in particular that are personal favorites?

There are many that I am proud to know I had a hand in creating. Starting with Mirrors ("Shirley", "Everything Near Me", "Annie", "I've Been Down") and RFTT ("So Cold", "What Love Is", "Ain't It Fun", "30 Seconds Over Tokyo", and of course "Final Solution"). Then with later bands that I formed when I left Cleveland like Saucers ("Muckraker", "A Certain Kind Of Shy", "What We Do") and The Bell System ("America Now", "You Be You") in Connecticut and The Down-fi ("Godot", "Don't Keep Me Waiting", "Let It Rain") here in Indiana. I am also happy to have had the opportunity to work with and play great songs in Deezen, The Gizmos, Simply Saucer (Edgar Breau's fantastic Canadian proto punk outfit), and X_____X with John Morton and Andrew Klimek (Jamie's youngest brother).

As the seventies and eighties progressed many bands who had drawn inspiration from the work you did with Mirrors and RFTT reached commercial and critical acceptance that you guys never had the opportunity to. Was their ever any bitterness about this and was it hard waiting for a number of archival releases to finally start to place the proper importance on what you all did?

This is a very rough business and there is no guarantee that anybody is going to have any success in it. I admire anyone who can find success and am honored to have them cite that what we have done previously was an inspiration for them. I am grateful that the effort we have put into it has been recognized to some extent and that I continue to have the opportunity to get out in front of an audience and play my music for them. That being said, I would like for it to have been us!

Before RFTT reunited in the nineties you were in a number of bands and put out quite a few releases. From that period, what stands out to you today as perhaps the most personal and powerful?

The years I spent in Connecticut, playing in bands and touring the region from 1977-1989 was a formative era in my life. My wife at that time was Rene Duer, who had moved with me to CT from Ohio and was instrumental in helping get my first band, Saucers, off the ground in 1977. She named the band, helped shape our image and did a tremendous job of designing our flyers and the cover art for our two singles.
I was a member in a number of bands, most of them I formed with many talented people starting with those that I met through placing ads in the paper looking to find a way into a new music scene, to meeting over the years of playing in the clubs of Southern New England. I am proud to have issued a compilation from those early days in 1982 on Gustav Records called *It Happened But Nobody Noticed*. The original LP contained 13 bands that represented the music scene we had created from '77-80 at our home, Ron's Place. Our own CBGBs on the edge of Yale University. In 2008, I re-released the original album on CD and at that time collected 13 more archival recordings of bands from that era in a second CD. There is also a YouTube documentary (2009) by the same title that was inspired by the re-release party.

On kind of a personal note, it is cool to see you have an Indiana connection. I live in Frankfort, Kentucky now but I went to high school just outside of Evansville, IN in a small town called Newburgh. Is your homebase still in the Indiana area?

I live in Indianapolis with my wife Claudia, and our two cats. We moved to Indiana from Connecticut in 1989. Claude had played bass in The Plan and The Bell System with me. We also have a side project called The Rhythm Methodists which started in 1988 with drummer Kerry Miller in New Haven. A few years ago, Kerry became a resident of Indianapolis and we have resurrected that band to record and have fun with.

How did it feel to reunite with Rocket From The Tombs in the late nineties and finally get a proper full-length release out? Was it difficult to get back into that groove after so many years had gone by and was the justified acclaim from both critics and fans rewarding?

It was amazing what happened with RFTT in the early '00s. I guess the seeds were planted in the late 1990's for our 2003 reunion show at UCLA. I was visiting Cleveland in 1996 when I saw David at Jim Jones' home. He played a tape Jim had made of our 1975 performance opening for Television at The Piccadilly in Cleveland. This was 20 years after the event and the first I knew of the recording's existence! David said he was considering cleaning it up and maybe putting something out someday. When I visited him while in England in 1999 I said that if he ever did consider putting the tapes from those days out, I hoped he would also consider having a reunion to go along with its release. At this time I had stopped playing music for nearly a decade and had only recently started to pick it back up. We would travel out to Columbus OH to do a Xmas benefit show with an old CT guitarist friend who had relocated to the center of Ohio. I was delighted see the release of *The Day The Earth Met Rocket From The Tombs* in 2002 and then for David to propose a reunion performance consisting of David, Cheetah, and myself along with Pere Ubu drummer Steven Mehlman and the great Richard Lloyd of Television in place of Peter.

That weekend in Los Angeles was memorable for a number of reasons, including the joy so many of the fans who had traveled from all over the world to be there expressed. Just before we were to start a couple of guys rushed up to me and asked if we had already gone on, and were relieved to hear they had just made it. "We just got off the plane from New Zealand!" they exclaimed!

I'm amazed by how tireless you are and how much you musically you are involved with. Which leads us to the remarkable X_____X. Were you aware of them when they first briefly formed in the late seventies and how did you come to join the band as it stands now?

John formed X_____X as a short-term band with Andrew, John Ellis, and Anton Fier in the summer of 1979. I became aware of them when Jim Jones wrote me a letter and mentioned that Johnny Dromette was releasing a single. I had that one and the other ordered by my friends at the record store in New Haven. John had moved to NYC by then but I never saw him there before I moved away in 1989. I reconnected with John in 2003 when his NYC band New Fag Motherfuckers opened for RFTT at The Village Underground. After that we did not see each other until John contacted me through Facebook in 2014 and asked me if I would be interested in joining a reformed X_____X to do some shows in support of a archival LP that was released on a label in Finland. John, Andrew, drummer Matt Harris and I played together for a handful of shows through the next few months and decided that we sounded good and should continue. Since then we have done quite a few tours and recorded our LP *Albert Ayler's Ghosts* live at the Yellow Ghetto in 2015. We are presently working to finish our next album *The Monster That Ate Cleveland* and by the spring a single will should be available on MME records.

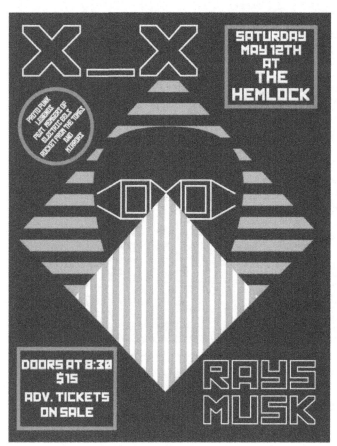

What is it like to work with John Morton?

John is a great artist and musician. He is a challenge to work with because he forces me to get out of my comfort zone and explore ideas I may not have chosen on my own. I appreciate that. John and I have known of each other since we were in Jr. High School in Lakewood. We ran in the same circles in High School and our respective bands, Mirrors, RFTT and electric eels played shows together; the eels also shared a rehearsal space with Rocket. Yet I did not play with John, or really get to know him until we started working together in X_____X; since then we have spent a lot of time together and I enjoy him as a bandmate and a friend as well as my long time admiration for his art.

Do you have more archival music in the vault that might someday get an official release and what are your thoughts on streaming services as opposed to physical media?

Besides the compilation CD mentioned above there are CDs available of Saucers original recordings that was released by GTA records in Los Angeles in 2002, My recent Indianapolis band released two CDs and two singles between 2009-2016 most of which are still available. In 2014 I released the LP *aka Darwin Layne* on ever/never records (NYC). This is a collection of recordings from Connecticut 1981-88 that had not seen release along with some earlier recordings 1974-79. Later this year (2018) will see a vinyl release of Saucers material, *Third Saucer from the Sun* on Rerun Records (St. Louis);

some tracks that were previously released on the 2002 CD as well as new material that was unearthed after the CD had been released. This includes a cut from a CD released in 2011 *2nd Saucer* that reunited members of Saucers to record material from our heyday that never made it onto tape at that time.

aka Darwin Layne

Craig Bell

Saucers and Down-fi material are also available for streaming or download on all the usual sites. I wish there was better compensation from these platforms, but I'm glad they are there for the listener to discover us.

You just recently wrapped up a tour with X_____X. Do you still enjoy playing live?

I love the shows, I loathe the drives between them. I do like to tour and to meet all the people who come out to the shows. I man the merch table so I am always glad to see our fans stop by.

Finally, are there any future hopes or plans you would like to share and where are the best spots online fans can keep up with you at?

Claudia and I, along with our webguy Karl Brandt put together a website, craigwbell. com and we hope you will stop by and check it out.
   I have been doing some shows as Craig Bell & Band for the past couple years and I hope to get the band into the studio and record some new songs these coming months.

FIND OUT MORE ABOUT CRAIG BELL AT CRAIGWBELL.COM

"Should enhance Roeg's reputation as a pioneer of eroticism on film"
—Bruce Williamson, Playboy

The Rank Organization Presents A NICOLAS ROEG FILM

BAD TIMING/A SENSUAL OBSESSION

ART GARFUNKEL   THERESA RUSSELL   HARVEY KEITEL   DENHOLM ELLIOTT in
BAD TIMING/A SENSUAL OBSESSION   Director of Photography Anthony Richmond
Director of Music Richard Hartley   Editor Tony Lawson   Associate Producer Tim Van Rellim
SCREENPLAY BY YALE UDOFF   PRODUCED BY JEREMY THOMAS
DIRECTED BY NICOLAS ROEG
A Recorded Picture Company Production   Filmed in Technovision   A W●RLD NORTHAL FILM
A Sondra Gilman/Louise Westergaard Presentation

RACING
RESULTS · OBITS
Los Angeles Times
WEDNESDAY
MORNING
FINAL

New Floods Batter Desert

Worst of Storm Still to
Come, Forecasters Say

PAUL SIMON

ONE-TRICK PONY

Rock & Roll will give you some laughs but it won't do you any favors.

One-Trick Pony

starring PAUL SIMON and BLAIR BROWN also starring RIP TORN , JOAN HACKETT,
ALLEN GOORWITZ , MARE WINNINGHAM , LOU REED
Produced by MICHAEL TANNEN   Co-Produced by MICHAEL HAUSMAN
Written by PAUL SIMON   Directed by ROBERT M. YOUNG   Original Music by PAUL SIMON

From Warner Bros. A Warner Communications Company

DOLBY STEREO
IN SELECTED THEATRES

R   RESTRICTED
UNDER 17 REQUIRES ACCOMPANYING
PARENT OR ADULT GUARDIAN

WRECK & ROLL:

AN INTERVIEW WITH

JOHN D. MORTON

BY JEREMY
R. RICHEY

SOLEDAD: Hi John. Thanks so much participating in this interview. I really appreciate your kindness and time. I'm originally from Kentucky and used to travel up through Cleveland a lot. What was it like growing up there in the fifties and sixties when there so much change going on in art, music, film and popular culture in general?

JOHN D. MORTON: The art culture was popularized in the movies and media of the time. So as I was born into that era, I didn't realize this was a rift from the old WWII that brought a lot of artists from euro to NYC. Being like 5 years old, I didn't know that fact.
I just saw the results.

There was one gallery in the Cleveland Art museum that had any kind of "modern" work. Museum director Sherman Lee had said that as long as he was director of the museum none of the museum walls would boast an Andy Warhol. Talk about provincial . . . I learned about modern art by subscribing to the art mags and once a month would get a glimmer of what was going on. I used to go to the art museum every weekend as a kid. The armor court—what boy from that era didn't love Knights? There was an odd small painting of John the Baptist's head on a plate, now that's way cool Daddy-o! I think I was drawn into the artistic culture because it was exciting and it was where my talents lied. My parents also encouraged it. My dad and I didn't play catch or go hunting, water skiing or fishing. He would take me to Clark's Restaurant where I would have coffee with a lot of milk and sugar. Then to Johnson and Sons Hardware to pick up whatever supplies for whatever Saturday "fix it" job was to take place around the house. We would take a walk in the woods in the Rocky River Valley, part of Cleveland's great metropolitan Parks. We had one great Saturday where we went to The Flats (Cleveland's industrial area with the steel mills and the Cuyahoga River). I saw huge iron bridges of every configuration, swing, turntable, lift, tilt. It is very impressive to see that engineering in action. Dreadnoughts!

Along with your incredible career in music you are also an accomplished artist and writer. I was curious what else turned you on to the arts as a kid?

As I mentioned, kids, (at least boys) back then wanted to grow up to be (at least in the '50s) a fireman or a policeman (it was too soon to be an astronaut). Myself, I wanted to be a steam locomotive. Not an engineer but a fuckin Choo Choo Train! I was very disappointed when I learned it was impossible to achieve my inanimate and non-sentient career goals. After being a steam locomotive, my second choice was volcano.
I was really influenced by popular culture. I remember listening to The Beatles on my Japanese transistor radio with the one earphone. TV! Maynard G. Krebs! Monster movies with scientists!
I don't know any of my peers who professed to wanting to be a CPA or an insurance salesman.
I was a real Junior Scientist; I was good at it . . . along with my conceived romanticized idea of what it was to be a "scientist." In more than one of the Ishirô Honda's Toho films, when faced with a kaiju of perplexing proportions the line that would be excitedly uttered at The Diet would be, "What do the Scientists say?"
In the fifth grade we started to actually go to classes aside from homeroom. Mr. Fiore Tassone was a really great science "teacher." He burst my romantic bubble the day he told the class that to be a scientist would not be bursting through the doors of the inner sanctum

with the white lab coat trailing behind my excited figure holding a beaker of some smoking and bubbling green chemical but to be a scientist one would duplicating experiments with hundreds of other scientists in some giant Pharma Giant corporation.

It was then that I decided to be an "artist." One could still proudly be autonomous, weird, hip, and socially mischievous in that avocation. I also really had chops in it. When I was in nursery school I drew crayon pictures of buildings in perspective. Not bragging, just true. I saw a building and a side at the same time so I drew it that way.

When I was 4 years old. My parents would drop me off at Sunday School at The Lakewood Congregational Church while they went to services. It was an otherworldly experience, the old silver-haired Sunday School teachers, the strange and scary pictures of smiling contented bearded shepherds in clothes that looked like bathrobes and sheep and fucking donkeys!

The worst and scariest was a cross about 4 feet tall just standing by itself on a stand on the floor in an unused room, but you could see it through the doorway as we walked to the classroom. It was the perfect size to crucify a four-year-old boy. I liked my five half days at nursery school, but Sunday School had these mores hanging in the air like the radioactive mist that shrunk the Incredible Shrinking Man. I knew the mores were there, but I did not know what the fuck they were or what the fuck I should do to placate them.

This one particular Sunday they (the silver-haired Sunday School teachers always worked in tandem) placed a plank paper and crayons at everyone's desk. This Sunday, at least, there would be no incomprehensible stories about fucking shepherds, evil Romans, that lummox Goliath and the tasteless Philistines. I was golden with crayons and paper! My fucking raison d'être, But what should I draw given the unfathomable mores? I decided a safe choice would be the church itself. It was a beautiful structure, red brick with portico frieze of two-story white Doric columns, tasty! Green ivy growing on the red brick. So I do my journeyman drawing of the church, but there something missing. It is static, nothing to suck the audience into the picture . . . to get them engaged. I know, I'll make it on fire! So I have red, yellow and orange flames gushing from the roof topped with absolutely beautiful black smoke! Next thing I know the drawing is snapped up from the desk faster than Master Kan eludes Caine with the pebble. I am summarily banished to the steps outside of the church where my father found me crying after services. I had no idea what I had done to transgress the mores, but I did know that I had somehow screwed the fucking cosmic pooch. Little I knew that this self-fucking would occur many times over again in my artistic life.

There is an assumption on my part that everyone know all the TV shows I watched growing up. *The Real McCoys, The Many Loves of Dobie Gillis, Kung Fu*. If you don't know them, it is your mandate to look them up. (Try Google or Wikipedia.)

I guess maybe "what drew me to the arts" answer is, it is the one thing I can do. I used to throw the shot. Maybe I had enough talent to do that in the Olympics . . .
but I picked up my $125 Kent electric guitar instead.

What type of music did you grow up with?
Any particular favorites your family had that made a big impression on you?

My parents lived in squaresville and listened to easy listening. They did have a singular *Jazz At Oberlin* by The Dave Brubeck Quartet but that was it. Listening to A.M. radio on summer vacations in Marblehead, Ohio one would brook a lot of Ray Conniff. I read Szwed's biography of Sun Ra; Sonny was purported to have an admiration for Conniff as Conniff was a great arranger, something that Ra had done for Fletcher Henderson. Well if Conniff was good enough for Le Sonny Ra, he was good enough for me. I own a quite a few hours of Conniff now much to the displeasure of my wife.

Growing up in Cle in those times, finding anything out of the norm was work. Lamp's Melody Lane, the records store in Lakewood that supplied Mom and Dad's canon of Herb Alpert and the Tijuana Brass finally tore out the listening booths and had a singular bin marked "Underground." In that I found, Fresh Cream and the ESP sampler #1 and The Fugs. Just shopping for music based on the cover art. The first Grateful Dead was there. I bought it . . . they can't all be winners.

My mother, the hero of all her own stories (I mean, who isn't really?) claims she tried out singing a tune on stage for Louis Prima at Chippewa Lake where her parents had a cottage. Knowing my mom I'm guessing as she was giving Mr. Prima a blowjob in his trailer before the gig and he prolly made promises he had no intention of granting. She got beat out by that horrible junkie, Keely Smith. That was my mom's standard designation for people who had cosmically offended her. Nick Adams, that horrible junkie, Sal Mineo, that horrible junkie, etc etc etc.

PS: I saw the local band, The Rationals (Ann Arbor) who had a regional hit with Respect at Chippewa Lake, though I did not try out for the band (or give any BJs).

I know that both literature and film were both influences on you.
What are some of your favorites and did you feel like your interest in more than just music helped inform your legendary band electric eels?

The eels didn't go out to be legendary. However we did, incorrectly, assume we would be very popular. The kids will LOVE it we thought and were sorely perplexed and saddened when that didn't transpire. Dave E. and I particularly honed our songwriting. We worked very hard to arrive at our music and in the end, the eels sounded exactly as we had wished. I went into the eels fully weaponized with every Burroughs, Kerouac, Camus, Gide book I read. Every Stockhausen, Partch, Bartok, Ives record I heard. With the films *Strangelove, Them, Gojira, The Mysterians, The Seventh Seal*, that I saw. Every Soft Machine, Sun Ra, Yardbirds, Hendrix, and Beefheart concert I had seen.

In an older interview I read with you, you mentioned that the idea of 'anti-music' was in place from the beginning of electric eels. How important is the idea of confrontational art to you in your music, writing and artwork?

I always believed that doing any kind of art work (literature, music, visual) was supposed to be pushing new boundaries. I had assumed that was actually an aesthetic tenet; I found out that was an incorrect assumption on my part, but it did work for me.

I used to spend vast amounts of time as a young artist formulating aesthetics. I wrote a set of artist's rules that included (among others; below not necessarily in hierarchical order)

1. Artists can hold two dichotomic points of view
in their mind at the same time.
(I like that word 'dichotomic' because it almost
has the word 'atomic' in it given my veneration of science).

2. Artists can shave with two razors at the same time.

3. Everything that I say is art, is art.

4. Artists can contradict themselves
(associated with rule #1).

5. Not really a rule,
but I had a rubber stamp I made up that said,
"This is Art!"

I felt that learning the scales and being technically proficient would get in the way of pure musicality. Similarly in art and writing. Ornette Coleman talked about playing the violin left-handed (he was right-handed) to remove the virtuosity away from the purity of music. I didn't know about this at the time, but I certainly agreed with it. I learned from Sun Ra (not literally, but from his music) There are NO wrong notes and there is NO wrong timing. I saw Sun Ra and the Arkestra at South Hampton High School Auditorium on a Sunday afternoon at 4 pm. It was after he had had his stroke. He was so enfeebled two Arkestrians had to walk him over to the piano and sit him down at the bench. The stroke had affected his left side, the rhythm side of the piano so he could only play about one fifth of the notes he used to, but those notes and the timing of them were out of this world, (which is an apt metaphor to use when discussing Sun Ra).
From all of this sprung the ideology of "anti." Thus kinda "anti" what existed. Thus kinda "anti-music'' that I dove headlong into the eels with.

I remember 25 years ago when I first read From The Velvets To The Voidoids I was struck by how the story of electric eels is basically the story of what would become known as punk and modern rock just years earlier...everything from the attitude to the sound to even the clothes. Was there ever any bitterness watching other artists and bands get credit for the look and sounds you guys created?

. . . yes

The artwork you created also predates a lot of the fanzine culture that would become so important throughout the seventies and eighties.
Were you creating promotional pieces to go along with your music from the get-go or did that come later?

I am not familiar with the term 'fanzine culture.' I always had concurrent visual ideas to go along with our music. I did make four-foot-tall corrugated cardboard silhouettes of dinosaurs for stage props in the eels (called 'Silly Wets' of course) Especially in X____X (and super-especially in Johnny and the Dicks) I liked to mix in some visual and performance art things. We still do Tool Jazz. In the organic analogue version during an X____X set I would pick up a corded rip saw and slice through a lengthy of 2 X 4 while Jim held a rip saw aloft with the trigger on. Now it's been updated to a cordless Sawzall® and a length of bamboo. (The bamboo is much more a microtonal sound when the cut-offs hit the stage.)
In 2015 we did it in Boston and when we finished the number the audience just stood there mute and all until I asked if they were forgetting something . . . then they started clapping.

You talk a bit about stuff like no wave, fanzine cultures. For instance, we didn't have the acronym DIY back then, we just did it ourselves (Colab was a perfect example of this).

An eighties era Colab Logo from collaborativeprojects.wordpress.com

Your website has some great examples of your incredible artwork. From photography to graphic design, do you have a preferred style that you most like working with?

It isn't that I am unaware of these genres or categories but those words don't really define ideas. I am like a luxury ocean liner with restaurants, pools, gambling, nightclubs, skeet shooting, saunas etc. I am not being vain here, but I am the deluxe art package cruise. I am a jack of all trades who does a lot amazingly well. Doing it well, however, does not necessarily translate into popularity or $s. As I am jumping around on this with the answers, I will touch on this more, further on.

I just do what I guess I am supposed to do. I get asked what kind of music I do. I usually answer that I do the kind of music that someone who did proto-punk music in the early 70's does now.

So I have to ask about Peter Laughner.
How did you first meet him, what was your working relationship like and now,
more than 40 years after his death,
how do you view his work as a musician and songwriter?

"Ain't it fun when you know you're gonna die young."

PETE LAUGHNER
Temporalworth High Steppers

Well, was it Peter?

Why not speak ill of the dead? Until he died, Peter was just
another jerk in the Clevo music scene (I proudly put myself in this same category of jerks). Unfortunately, the best thing Peter did for his career is to die.
If he were still around I am not persuaded
we would be discussing him
. . . then again we might.

EVERY MONDAY NIGHT AT
THE OAR HOUSE
the corner of E. 21st & Chester
18 and over
NO COVER CHARGE

'For those of you who no longer cast your eyes heavenward
save through the bottom of an empty bottle'
Charles Baudelaire

I've heard most of the archival stuff working on a forever forthcoming release on Smog Veil Records and I heard him live in many guises (Rocket from the Tombs, Cinderella Backstreet, Friction,
Peter and the Wolves,
Mr. Stress
and solo gigs with vocals and acoustic).

Peter was an ok guitar player with an ok distinctive voice. A lot of his stage persona was simply embarrassing. Singing like a Lou Reed clone in a vinyl jumpsuit? (Couldn't Lou afford leather?) Peter never really had the chance to become something,
Death can do that.

Craig and I were on stage at The Painted Lady in Detroit on the second gig of our first ever X___X tour in 2014. Craig asides to me, "Today is Peter's birthday." I felt so sad. Peter should have been on stage with us, or in the audience or not in the audience because he was too busy with work after assuming command of his Dad's Biz Luke Laughner Packing Tape Supplies, Maintenance and Dispensers, but he wasn't any of those things. He was just dead.

I didn't realize at the time what a profound effect Peter's death would have on me. I didn't put together that I started my art project of suicide notes soon after in reaction to his death. Self-awareness isn't one of my strengths. I was suffering from deep depression and PTSD (just like "punk" they didn't have a name for it back then) and had suicidal ideation without fully realizing it. Self-medicating with copious amounts of alcohol and drugs. The big difference between me and Peter is I didn't die.

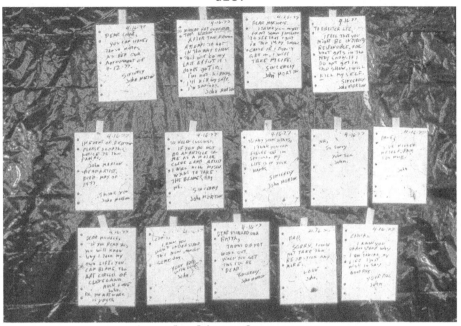

(couple lines from notes:
"Dad,
Sorry, I could not take the rejection anymore.
Love John"

"Dear Ma,
See note to Dad.
John")

I am glad you are talking to Craig
because I know he has a different take on Peter.

The story of X___X is just as fascinating as electric eels.
Did you feel an affinity for the No Wave movement of the late seventies when you first started the band?

Punk, proto-punk, new wave, no wave . . . those are all terms designated by others, the press, the biz, not by musicians (except maybe Green Day . . .). WE were however so very prescient in the eels! Self-declaring ourselves as proto-punk years before they invented the term punk.
There wasn't the term "no wave" back then. Sire Records' Seymour Stein decided "punk" was too aggressive a nomenclature so he coined new wave which we thought was so despicable, desperate and lame we started using the term no wave. I don't know if we coined the term but I do know we were using it before we heard it elsewhere.

I never felt affinity for anything. I didn't identify with any group. When someone complained about Philip Guston giving up the flag of abstract expressionism, Willem de Kooning said, "Why shouldn't he? It's not like we're a baseball team!" I was just doing my (and our) music. It is actually quite a laugh that we are a new band doing (for the most part) new music under the banner of a group that lasted 6 months 34 years ago.

I'm really intrigued by COLAB and your work there.
Can you tell us a bit about that
and the other work in art, music and literature you were doing in this period?

When I was agonizing about moving to NYC (I had thought I could have a career as a Cleveland artist. NOT SO) a friend and mentor Richard Van Buren said, "at least in NYC you'll have a place to show." I thought he meant a 57th Street gallery, what he meant is that Colab would break into a city-owned building on Houston Street and mount an exhibition called "A Real Estate Show" in which I would participate.

Original poster by Becky Howland
For more on the Real Estate Show please visit
placesjournal.org/article/where-can-we-be-123-delancey-street/

Two days after the opening the city came in and confiscated all the artwork except mine because they couldn't figure out how to get it through the door. Josef Beuys came down with that hat and the New York Times: "Hey! Let the kids have their show!"
I was treated a bit as a feral being . . . as a fauvist in Colab (and in fact by almost any institution I have run across).
They wouldn't let me use the indoor bathroom at the Colab meetings and I would have to go outside to piss in the street
(OK, a slight exaggeration . . .)

When we eels finished one of our handful of gigs, an audience member came up to me and said, "You guys are wrong!" Not, "Your music sucks!" Not "You're too loud!" Not "You guys are unprofessional!" but "You guys are WRONG!"

Despite the fact that I had a term as "president" of Colab, there is no picture of the group with me in it. I had to put my own name as a member on the Colab Wikipedia page. I guess I am talking here about the way I have been treated in general by the arts community. My second wife, a mover and shaker in the NYC art world, Holly Block, insisted that I hide the book I was reading at the time from her cohort art muckety-mucks when we were in an exclusive arts retreat in Italy. (She was the invitee and I was the husband.) She thought the book might sully her reputation with the Art World Nabobs. The book was *The Complete Richard Allen, Vol 1 Skinhead, Suedehead. Skinhead Escapes.*

Scott Billingsley was also involved with COLAB.
I'm a big fan of the No Wave cinema movement and love his work with Beth B.
Did you stay connected to the world of cinema as your own work in art and music progressed?

1981: Glenn O'Brien invited me to do a cameo in the movie he wrote, *New York Beat*. He enticed me with the carrot, "All the dope I could wish for!" would be had. (I got a $50 check which translated into NOT all the dope I could wish for.) I was to play a bouncer keeping Jean Michele Basquiat out of the Peppermint Lounge night club. My line was something like, "No! No you can't go in . . ." then I get distracted and Jean-Michele gets by me. The first take and Glenn says I was smiling. I often smile before I hurt someone, I replied. Did another nonsmiling take. Glenn called me that night after he saw the rushes. "Jeeze John! You can actually act! You have a film presence!" So I'm figuring, once the film comes out, I can be a character actor playing heavies . . . playing lugs! Of course, the financing for the movie falls apart and the footage goes to Italy where they lose the soundtrack. It is not released until 2001 under the title *Downtown 81*
(which is how I know what year this story is set!).

I saw *The American Friend*. The only movie I saw during the '80s. I believe I have answered the question as to loving the no wave cinema.

You have worked a lot with internet design.
What are your thoughts on social media and the way that the internet has changed the way we interact with each other?
Also what are your thoughts on
streaming vs. physical media when it comes to music and film?

For musicians, the music business has always sucked. With the internet it sucks even more faster. No one has to pay for music. I have nothing against the ease of use and immediacy of streaming. I did all of the audio and artwork for X STICKY FINGERS X over the internet (see Ektro below). I am never impressed by computers. Just zeros and ones. They do great handy things, for instance, I would have never had an opportunity to contact my first wife, the artist Michele Zalopany. I knew she lived at the Chelsea but I would never have phoned her, written to her or have sent an email, but because of handy dandy Facebook we know have a renewed relationship. Facebook tells me when it is someone's birthday, even dead people who still exist in the data world. But all that stuff

. . . it is just mechanics. To quote David McCallum in the *Outer Limits (The Sixth Finger)* when asked if he could play the piano before, "It's just mathematics." I don't give a fuck about analog or digital. I have this running joke about trying to lift a Pono to go jogging with my 6 (that's all that can fit on The Pono) lossless music files. (It's a visual, if you could see me mime-straining under the weight of The Pono now you'd be laughing your fucking ass off.) I am certainly not a Luddite, I actually am facile around computers, but technology is just technology and technology is NOT art.

What led you to reigniting X___X and how does this version of the band compare to the one that briefly appeared in 1978?

In 2014 I was approached by Ektro Records, a not-for-profit record company in Finland as to re-releasing the original two Drome singles. That culminated in a full length archival release, *X STICKY FINGERS X.* When I finished all the work I just toyed with the idea of a support tour. Andrew Klimeyk and Anton Fier were on board but Jim Ellis declined so I went through my list of bass players. Craig was the one on the list who accepted. Then Tony dropped out. I was three days away from canceling the tour when this kid, Matthew "B.T.A." Harris showed up. (I nicknamed him, it stands for Better Than Anton). We all went to Craig's home in Indianapolis and practiced in his basement studio for three days and hit the road. On the way from Chicago to the last gig in Cle Andrew had booked us a couple hours at Negative Space Recording Studio where we recorded four songs in two hours. That recording ended up selling Smog Veil Records on a deal as long as it included Albert Ayler's *Ghosts* which none of us knew but I had only talked about recording it as an idea.
Since then, as I mentioned earlier, we are basically a new band treading merrily along with an old name. That fact keeps us touring, recording (and designing and selling merch!)
How does the 2014 X___X compare to the 1978?
It is defiantly comparable to any of the other bands that lasted (by design) for 6 months and picked up again after a 36 year hiatus.

Do you enjoy touring and playing live and what kind of experience do you like to give an audience coming to see you?

Playing live gigs is our job #1. It is the only viable means to stay alive as a band in the current music echelon for music like ours. There is no money to be made from recording. Artist Robert Sikora saw us in Cle in 2014 and when he saw us two years later in Cleveland he said, "You guys are a MONSTER!" Robert's valuation gave us the title of our next release, *The Monster that Ate Cleveland.* In the 60's sitcom *The Many loves of Dobie Gillis*, Bob "Gilligan" Denver co-stars as Dobie's beatnik buddy, Maynard G. Krebs, who keeps suggesting they go down to The Bijou to catch *The Monster that Devoured Cleveland* (or its sequel, *Son of the Monster that Devoured Cleveland.*) I just liked "Ate" better. We really are where we are meant to be when we are on stage and performing. I spent years in the eels rehearsing; that was like prison.
We give it 110% (some nights 120% [why I am not a math professor]).
Judging by audience response, we kill it consistently.
I love meeting these kid musicians (well, a thirty-year-old is "kids" to us). We have a communication between us that is music.
It is charming!

How did you reconnect with Craig Bell
and what is it like working with him?

I don't know if I would call it "reconnecting" with Craig. While we went to high school together and while he played bass (the eels never had a bass player) he played in that other band . . . Mirrors. So it is like we were meant to wind up doing this in our 60s. We really work well together as friends, musicians and as a business model. I had toured a total of 17 days in the entirety of my musical career up until 2014, Craig has been on the road quite a lot comparatively. Craig is the road manager and I am maybe the artistic director. One of us is the remora and the other the shark, but I can never be certain which one is which.

Finally are there any particular future projects you'd like to share with us and where are the best spots online that fans can keep up with you and your work?

I seem like a contrarian in this interview, but I never really have any 'future projects'. I just kinda keep working. As a band we will certainly keep recording and gigging. We don't retire. I am always open to playing with other musicians. I certainly will continue making art. I am writing my roman à clef memoirs to be published by Hozac Books in 2019. I just got a gig doing a record cover for a kid band, Urochromes. I really like the music (otherwise I'd never do it for the paltry $s they can pay). I really love doing record covers and the record covers I do are because people want me, John D Morton, as an artist. That is so way-cool to me. (You like me, you really like me!) I plan to continue working at anything and I have no real idea beyond, maybe six months, where my spiritual/artistic path will take me. I heard an idea expressed once, "If you know the destination of your spiritual path don't bother going on it." I hold to that. God, in whom I do not believe, gave me these abilities and I am ever grateful to be able to use them. Not much money; I have made more money in art and music in the last three years than in the entirety of my prior career and I am just now reaching sub-subsistence economically.

I guess to describe myself in a summarization I'm just a fellow that read *On The Road* at 14, was abused physically and sexually by my mother (that's why I have a tattoo of a black heart with a swastika in it with the first line of Camus *The Stranger* in French in a beautiful banner in script. For many years the Stuart Gilbert, the Bad Translator wrote the first line from whence the whole existential ballgame unfolds as "Mother died today" when a more accurate rendering would be "Mommy died today." Two very different psychological starting points. So the tat is about my black-hearted Nazi mother. The first time my sister, who is Jewish, saw it she said, "Well you finally went and did it. You got a swastika tattoo!" I said, "It's about Mom!" She said, "I know, that's obvious!"

I am bipolar, another thing they didn't have a name for back then (is it odd that I own a copy of the D.S.M.?) Bipolar with transient psychotic symptoms. I wrote the song "Transmography" about how (when I am in a transient psychotic state) people's faces transmography, usually into something unpleasant and frightening like a gargoyle. Luckily I—I was able to interpret these feelings correctly. Loss of essence.

I self-medicated with alcohol and drugs.

My topic for my fifth grade thesis was Heroin,

the research done mostly from the *Life* magazine
article that later became the basis for the screenplay, *The Panic in Nee-dle Park*. And being *Life* magazine it was chock full of wonderful
pictures black and white photos of "junkies" using the "works" to inject
the "horse" into their arms in order to get their "fix!"
The photo of the heroin heroine (I couldn't resist) in her hospital bed
to in order to "kick" her habit looked very much like my mother did the
first thing in the morning after attending a suburban "party" with LOTS of
drinks and not removing her eye make up before sleep.

L to R: Lamont Thomas, Andrew Klimeyk, John D Morton,
Craig Bell.   Photo cred: Jim O'Bryan

I got sober (23 years).

I was able to somewhat deal with my demons and
I am still alive and still on the stage and in the art studio.

What more could one want?

You can catch me and us at x—x.co.uk & mortonia.com
(I do have Paul-Marotta-is-a-Nazi.com and Brian-McMahon-is-a-Scum-bag.com but there isn't much on those sites.
I just use them to keep the email names alive for when I have to contact them to do electric eels business.)

0.5 OK, Extra question.
My wife asked me why I was getting up so early. I said I had to work on the *Soledad* interview.
She smiled and asked,
"If you were a tree, what kind of tree would you be?"

My answer: "The Fuck Off tree!"

LE GRAIN DE LA VOIX DANS LE MONDE ANGLOPHONE ET FRANCOPHONE,

EDITED BY MICHAËL ABECASSIS, MARCELLINE BLOCK, GUDRUN LEDEGEN, AND MARIBEL PEÑALVER VICEA

(BERN, BERLIN, BRUXELLES, FRANKFURT AM MAIN, NEW YORK, OXFORD, WIEN: PETER LANG, MODERN FRENCH IDENTITIES, 2018).
WE GRATEFULLY ACKNOWLEDGE PETER LANG PUBLISHING FOR GRANTING PERMISSION TO PUBLISH THIS EXCERPT.

MICHAËL ABECASSIS, MARCELLINE BLOCK, GUDRUN LEDEGEN, MARIBEL PEÑALVER VICEA, EDS.,
LE GRAIN DE LA VOIX DANS LE MONDE ANGLOPHONE ET FRANCOPHONE

(BERN, BERLIN, BRUXELLES, FRANKFURT AM MAIN, NEW YORK, OXFORD, WIEN: PETER LANG, MODERN FRENCH IDENTITIES, 2018).

Excerpt from The Voices Project

The Project on French Voices offers more than 60 entries written by academics about the memorable voices of influential people in the francophone world. Each entry—whether about an actor/actress, a singer, a journalist or a politician—describes the particular features that made these voices so distinctive and important. The voice is in itself a great source of information, as Bailblé puts it:

De l'être du sujet : sexe, âge, identité : origine socio-culturelle et empreinte vocale particulière (voice print) ; typage (façon de poser la voix, accents, habitudes articulatoires) mais aussi timbre de voix personnelle. 1
[About the being of the subject: sex, age, identity: socio-cultural origin and particular voice print; typing (way of posing the voice, accents, articulatory habits) but also the personal timbre of one's voice.]

Through the voice, it is not only a person that expresses himself/herself, but a different entity that exists on its own in our collective memory.

Gaston Bachelard (1884-1962)
By Michaël Abecassis, the University of Oxford
(Translated from the French by Marcelline Block)

The philosopher Gaston Bachelard was born in the small village of Bar-sur-Aube in Champagne-Ardenne. The rare video recordings of him that remain—those of an old man with a bushy white beard, sitting in the middle of piles of books—have made him the archetypal philosopher in the collective imagination. Listening to his unusual gravelly voice, marked by a pronounced Burgundy accent replete with the rolling "r," evokes a surreal quality that nurtured the collective imagination; in this sense, it is in itself an invitation to dream.

Sidonie-Gabrielle Colette (1873-1954)
By Michaël Abecassis, The University of Oxford
(Translated from the French by Marcelline Block)

Sidonie-Gabrielle Colette was born in the family birthplace of Saint-Sauveur-en-Puisaye, a village in Bourgogne. She possessed the husky, gravelly voice of a peasant, rolling the Burgundian "r," as evidenced by the rare recordings that remain of her voice. Louis Aragon associates this voice with the Bourgogne wine terroir in a poem that he wrote the day after her death: "with all the varietals of a Beaune/The rolling of the 'r' like a bottle of wine in the cellar."

Jean D'Ormesson (1925-2018)
By Michaël Abecassis, The University of Oxford

Jean D'Ormesson was above all a voice and a presence emanating from every television set. Born to an haute bourgeois Parisian family as Count Jean Bruno Wladimir Francois-de-Paule Lefèvre, he was elected to the Académie Française in 1970. An exceptional orator, with sparkling blue eyes and a benevolent smile playing on his lips, he elegantly wielded the passé simple and the imperfect subjunctive. He spoke eloquently and with an affectation in his voice that seemed charmingly old-fashioned, as if it belonged to another era. Despite what he said, describing himself jocularly as "ringard" (out of fashion)2, his persistently young and dynamic wit was very much in line with his times. These conversations had something of a timeless quality. Addressing himself to imaginary interlocutors, he brought to his conversations the greatest names in literature, a joyous erudition that left no spectator indifferent.

Jean-Pierre Marielle (1932-): "A voice that is 'reconnaissable entre mille' "
By Marcelline Block

Throughout his successful career on stage and screen spanning more than six decades, with appearances in over 100 films, Jean-Pierre Marielle's signature as an actor is his unmistakable voice — its deep, rich and resonant velvety timbre — which, when he made his onscreen debut in the 1950s, allowed him to incarnate characters who were more advanced in age than him. Whether in Bertrand Tavernier's Coup de Torchon (1981), Alain Corneau's Tous les matins du monde (1991), Chantal Akerman's Demain on déménage (2004), or Jean-Pierre Jeunet's Micmacs à tire-larigot (2009), Marielle has made his mark onscreen with his inimitable voice, which has been labelled "reconnaissable entre mille"3 such as those of Michel Bouquet and Louis Jouvet (Ibid). Marielle's instantly recognizable voice was heard in a radio advertisement for Père Magloire Calvados, which aired on RTL and Europe 1 in December 2013. He also lent his voice to films including the French versions of the BBC production Pride (John Downer, 2004) and Pixar's beloved Ratatouille (Brad Bird/Jan Pinkava, 2007) as well as L'Apprenti Père Noël (Luc Vinciguerra, 2010) and Phantom Boy (Jean-Loup Felicioli/Alain Gagnol, 2015). Beyond radio, film, and theatre, however, perhaps the best way to truly appreciate, enjoy, and fully experience the unforgettable quality of Marielle's iconic voice is to listen to him reading his own words in the audiobook version of his autobiography, Le Grand n'importe quoi (Paris: Éditions Calmann-Lévy, 2010), in which he discusses, among other topics, his passion for jazz.

Henri Salvador

Henri Salvador (1917-2008)

By Marcelline Block

Iconic French singer and songwriter Henri Salvador's influence was felt across continents and encompassed numerous musical and performative genres as well as venues. Among his honors and awards from France are the Legion of Honor and National Order of Merit.

Salvador—a "velvet-voiced, Nat King Cole-like crooner and jazz guitarist"[4]—was born in Cayenne, French Guiana in 1917; his family moved to Paris during his childhood. This is where Salvador encountered jazz and taught himself to play the guitar, embarking upon his career in music while he was still an adolescent by performing in concert halls in Paris.

Salvador performed not only on stage—at famed Parisian theatres and music halls such as the Alhambra, ABC, and Bobino—but also in film and particularly on television during the 1960s and 70s. Furthermore, Salvador is credited, alongside his frequent songwriting collaborator Boris Vian (1920-1959) with bringing rock n' roll to France in the 1950s. In addition, Salvador was influential upon Latin American and Brazilian music, especially the Bossa Nova.

Salvador has been described as possessing a "silken" and "honeyed" voice; of his voice, Salvador himself stated that, "'I don't sing, I whisper….When you whisper into the mike, you are able to transmit real feeling.'"[5] Indeed, this is demonstrated by the fact that Salvador "was adored by an immense public, and especially by the young. It was natural, his songs were sensitive and delicate. He sang….with a tender, caressing, melancholy voice – he expressed better than anyone the essence of that generation."[6] These qualities of Salvador's voice come through beautifully in his iconic children's song "Une Chanson douce" (1950; lyrics by Maurice Pon).

Salvador's well-known penchant for exuberant laughter led to his nickname "Monsieur Joie-de-Vivre."[7] In Quincy Jones' estimation, "With Henri I've learnt that a big laugh is a really loud noise from the soul saying, 'Ain't that the truth?'"[8]

Salvador died in early February 2008 at age 90, a few months after giving his farewell concert in December 2007 at Le Palais des Congrès in Paris.

1. Claude Bailblé, «Programmation de l'écoute 3», Cahiers du cinéma 297 (février 1979): 53.

2. Jean-Claude Vantroyen, "Jean d'Ormesson au «Soir» en 2016 : «Je suis un ringard qu'on applaudit»," Le Soir, 29 January 2016, http://plus.lesoir.be/23527/article/2016-01-29/jean-dormesson-au-soir-en-2016-je-suis-un-ringard-quon-applaudit#.

3. Bernard Loupias, "L'abécédaire de Jean-Pierre Marielle," Le Nouvel observateur, 17 September 2010, http://bibliobs.nouvelobs.com/documents/20100916.BIB5640/l-039-abecedaire-de-jean-pierre-marielle.html.

4. Pierre Perrone, "Henri Salvador: France's 'Monsieur Joie de Vivre,'" The Independent, February 14, 2008, https://www.independent.co.uk/news/obituaries/henri-salvador-frances-monsieur-joie-de-vivre-781981.html.

5. IBID

6. Patrick O'Connor, "Obituary: Henri Salvador," The Guardian, February 18, 2008, https://www.theguardian.com/music/2008/feb/18/obituaries.france.

7. Peter Culshaw, "Seduced by Monsieur Joie-de-Vivre," The Telegraph, March 24, 2007, https://www.telegraph.co.uk/culture/music/rockandjazzmusic/3663970/Seduced-by-Monsieur-Joie-de-Vivre.html.

8. IBID

MARCELLINE BLOCK (BA, HARVARD; MA, PRINCETON; PHD CANDIDATE, PRINCETON) IS LECTURER IN HISTORY AT PRINCETON. SHE HAS EDITED, AND APPEARED IN, MANY BOOKS WHICH CAN BE SEEN AT AMAZON.COM/MARCELLINE-BLOCK/E/B002WWLQI4. FOLLOW HER AT TWITTER AT @MARCELLINEBLOCK

"MAGNIFICENT... OUTSTANDING... HEARTFELT...
A FANTASTIC PIECE OF CINEMA"

"FUNNY ... ENTERTAINING ... SEXY ... PROVOCATIVE"

★★★★★ ★★★★★ ★★★★ ★★★★

Amanda by Night

STARRING THE
NEW SENSATION **VERONICA HART** AS AMANDA

WITH SAMANTHA FOX • LISA DELEEUW • JAMIE GILLIS • RICHARD BOLLA
ARCADIA LAKE • BROOKE WEST • ERIC EDWARDS
WITH MAI LIN AND NICOLE NOIR • A FILM BY HAROLD LIME • IN COLOR

NOW SHOWING

HOYTS DRIVE-INS

| ALTONA | DONCASTER | WANTIRNA | M'BYRNONG |
| PRESTON | COBURG | OAKLEIGH | BURWOOD |

SNACK BARS 6·30 MOVIES 7·30
PROGRAMME INFORMATION TEL. 11680

PLUS, AT HOYTS DRIVE INS ONLY: "THE SEX MACHINE" (R)

ALSO AT MELBOURNE—CITY PROPER

THE PALACE
20 BOURKE ST. 662 2688
D'LY 3.15, 5.30, 8.00—NOT SUNDAY

GEELONG
VILLAGE STAR
DRIVE-IN

He has been working
for this moment
his entire life.
This is his last chance.
For her,
this could be the beginning.

THE COMPETITION

They broke the cardinal rule
of the competition...they fell in love

COLUMBIA PICTURES Presents
A RASTAR/WILLIAM SACKHEIM PRODUCTION
RICHARD DREYFUSS
AMY IRVING LEE REMICK
"THE COMPETITION"
SAM WANAMAKER

Original Music by LALO SCHIFRIN Story by JOEL OLIANSKY and WILLIAM SACKHEIM Screenplay by JOEL OLIANSKY
Produced by WILLIAM SACKHEIM Directed by JOEL OLIANSKY From RASTAR ☐☐ DOLBY STEREO PG PARENTAL GUIDANCE SUGGESTED ◁▷
IN SELECTED THEATRES SOME MATERIAL MAY NOT BE SUITABLE FOR CHILDREN

© 1980 COLUMBIA PICTURES INDUSTRIES, INC.

A Ghost From a Summer's Past:
Sarah Colvin photographed in Frankfort, Ky. by Jeremy R Richey

DRINK FULL, AND DESCEND: THE VIOLENT YET FLAMMABLE WORLD OF TWIN PEAKS

BY TARA HANKS

"It is happening again," David Lynch and Mark Frost tweeted on October 6, 2014. Their pet project, *Twin Peaks*, had been off the air for almost a quarter-century. A nine-episode series was set for broadcast on Showtime in 2016. But by April 2015, budget negotiations had broken down. "*Twin Peaks* may still be very much alive at Showtime," Lynch reflected. "I love the world of *Twin Peaks* and wish things could have worked out differently." Members of the original cast swiftly recorded a viral video, each speaking in character: "*Twin Peaks* without David Lynch is like pie without cherries." Almost 30,000 fans signed a Change.org petition, "SAVE *TWIN PEAKS!*" A month later, Showtime confirmed that Lynch was back on board – and the length of the 'limited event' would ultimately extend to eighteen hour-long episodes.

Among the returning cast are Mädchen Amick (as RR diner waitress Shelly), Dana Ashbrook (Bobby Briggs), Richard Beymer (Ben Horne), Sherilyn Fenn (Audrey Horne), Harry Goaz (Chief Deputy Andy Brennan), Michael Horse (Chief Deputy Hawk), David Patrick Kelly (Jerry Horne), Sheryl Lee (Laura Palmer), Peggy Lipton (Norma Jennings), David Lynch (Gordon Cole), James Marshall (James Hurley), Kyle MacLachlan (Dale Cooper), Everett McGill (Ed Hurley), Kimmy Robertson (Lucy Brennan), Wendy Robie (Nadine Hurley), Al Strobel (The One-Armed Man), Russ Tamblyn (Dr. Lawrence Jacoby), Alicia Witt (Gersten Hayward), and Grace Zabriskie (Sarah Palmer.)

There are also cameo appearances by others from the original cast, including Phoebe Augustine (Ronette Pulaski), Jan D'Arcy (Sylvia Horne), David Duchovny (Denise Bryson), Mark Frost (as reporter Cyril Pons), Warren Frost (Dr. Will Hayward), Andrea Hays (RR waitress Heidi), Gary Hershberger (Mike Nelson), Charlotte Stewart (Betty Briggs), and Ray Wise (Leland Palmer.) Notable absences include Michael Ontkean (Sheriff Harry Truman), now retired from acting, and replaced by Robert Forster as Harry's brother, Frank. Donna Hayward, the best friend of Laura Palmer played by Lara Flynn Boyle – and by Moira Kelly in the spin-off movie, Twin Peaks: Fire Walk With Me – is not part of the new series; but in *The Final Dossier*, Mark Frost reveals that Donna has finally reconciled with her father, 'Doc' Hayward. Frost also suggests that sawmill owner Catherine Martell (Piper Laurie) went into seclusion after her husband's death. Michael J. Anderson, aka The Man From Another Place, is replaced by The Evolution of The Arm, a tree-like entity topped with a clay head, and possessed of its own doppelganger.

Among the new faces are Jane Adams (Constance Talbot), Chrysta Bell (Tammy Preston), Jim Belushi (Bradley Mitchum), Laura Dern (Diane Evans), Eamon Farren (Richard Horne), George Griffith (Ray Monroe), Jennifer Jason Leigh (Chantal Hutchens), Ashley Judd (Beverly Paige), Robert Knepper (Rodney Mitchum), Caleb Landry Jones (Steven Burnett), Matthew Lillard (Bill Hastings), Don Murray (Bushnell Mullins), Joy Nash (Senorita Dido), John Pirrucello (Chad Broxford), Adele René (Lieutenant Cynthia Knox), Tim Roth (Gary 'Hutch' Hutchens), Amanda Seyfried (Becky Burnett), Amy Shiels (Candie), Tom Sizemore (Anthony Sinclair), Jake Wardle (Freddie Sykes), Naomi Watts (Janey-E Jones), Nae Yuki (Naido), Christophe Zajac-Denek (Ike 'the Spike' Stadtler.) Inevitably, some of the original cast are now deceased, including Don Davis (Major Garland Briggs) and Frank Silva (Killer Bob.) David Bowie, who declined to reprise his role as Phillip Jeffries in *Fire Walk With Me*, passed away in 2016. Nonetheless, their characters have a spectral presence in the new series. Catherine Coulson, a lifelong friend of Lynch, died just days after filming her scenes as Margaret Lanterman (aka 'The Log Lady.') Miguel Ferrer (Albert Rosenfield), and Harry Dean Stanton (Carl Rodd) also passed away after the show aired, as did Brent Briscoe (Dave Macklay) and Marvin Rosland (RR cook Toad.)

Lynch and Frost have also retained much of the original production team, including cinematographer Peter Deming, editor Duwayne Dunham, composer Angelo Badalamenti, casting director Johanna Ray, and now executive producer Sabrina Sutherland. The first two episodes were screened together at the Cannes Film Festival in May 2017, ahead of the TV premiere. After the screening, Lynch was given a standing ovation. He was visibly emotional, perhaps remembering past triumphs and defeats, not least the hostile reception that *Fire Walk With Me* once suffered. The show's run was flanked by the release of two epistolary novels by Mark Frost: *The Secret History of Twin Peaks*, and *Twin Peaks: The Final Dossier*.

Doesn't Get Any Bluer

The opening episode takes us back to the final moments of the original series, with Laura Palmer telling Dale Cooper, "I'll see you in twenty-five years." We return to the 'red room,' that liminal space connecting Twin Peaks with the spirit world and its 'lodges' of darkness and light. We then revisit other past signifiers, from the old sawmill to the high school, where a distressed young girl runs across the playground; and Laura's prom queen portrait is shown encased in the lobby. The following scene is in black and white, with an older Cooper listening to the spirit formerly known as The Giant. "Listen to the sounds," he tells Cooper, as a needle skips on the gramophone (recalling the noise of a stuck record as Leland Palmer murdered his niece, Maddy Ferguson.) "It is in our house now," he adds. "It

all cannot be said aloud now." As before, his speech is phonetically reversed. He tells Cooper to "remember 4-3-0 … Richard and Linda … two birds with one stone." This scene will be revisited in the final episode, as time is on a loop in Twin Peaks.

We are then transported to New York City, where a young man called Sam (Ben Rosenfield) sits in a large warehouse, looking into a glass box. In a metaphor for our own viewing experience, the camera pans around the room and we're left wondering what Sam's purpose may be. As he leaves the room to greet an obliging young woman named Tracey (Madeline Zima), it becomes clear that Sam is none the wiser. Tracey brings coffee in two paper cups marked 'Szymon's' – a brand we shall see more of. In Twin Peaks, characters often bond over coffee – but here, it's a prelude to seduction. Is she here to flirt with Sam, or to spy? After politely refusing to take her into the room, he opens the door, and catches her peeking: "You're a bad girl, Tracey!"

She returns later on with more coffee, and after buzzing Sam, notices the security guard has left. Sam talks a little more about his job, explaining that the building is owned by an anonymous billionaire. He leads Tracey inside, and they sit on the couch. It's a science experiment, he says, adding that the guy he replaced "saw something." After watching the box for a few moments, Tracey strips off and straddles Sam. Their embrace will be echoed in later sex scenes, with a tall, leggy woman always on top. Sam notices a shadowy form in the glass box and warns Tracey. She turns around and they huddle close as the glass shatters, and the entity known as 'The Experiment' escapes. Like characters in a slasher movie, the lovers are spattered with blood and their heads blown off.

It's daytime in Buckhorn, South Dakota. As Marjorie

Green (Melissa Bailey) approaches her apartment, her dog Armstrong sniffs at a neighbour's door. The smell is so foul that Marjorie panics and calls the police. Her neighbour, librarian Ruth Davenport, hasn't been seen for days, she tells them. The officers go outside and spot a rather shifty workman, Hank, carrying a large sack down an alley. Marjorie runs downstairs, having found her spare key. Marjorie's ditzy demeanour is reminiscent of Heidi, waitress at the RR Diner – and as the show's other fictional town, Buckhorn supplies a quirky counterpoint to Twin Peaks. The officers leave a bewildered Hank pleading, "Am I free to go?"

They are soon joined by Detective Dave Macklay and pathologist Constance Talbot, who enter Ruth's blue-walled apartment to find her severed head on the bed – and a headless male body under the covers. Back at the police station, Constance examines prints found in the apartment and traces them to William Hastings, her kid's high school principal. Macklay, who has known Hastings all his life, drives to his suburban home. On Hastings' door is a wolf-shaped knocker. His wife Phyllis answers, protesting, "But the Morgans are coming for dinner!" as hapless Bill is led away.

In the wilds of Dakota, Cooper's long-haired, leather-clad doppelganger – the 'Bad Cooper' who escaped from the lodge years ago, also played by Kyle MacLachlan – drives to a slowed-down version of Muddy Magnolias' 'American Woman,' its distorted vocals channelling the dark, menacing aesthetic of *Lost Highway*, Lynch's 'fugue state' thriller. Cooper's double arrives at a cabin in the woods where – after striking down an unlucky redneck who stands in his way – he is greeted by a criminal associate, Otis (Redford Westwood), as 'Mr C.' Among the cabin's other residents is Buella (Kathleen Deming), a tall woman with a strange, misshapen face. "Have you got them back there somewhere?" Mr. C asks. Ray Monroe appears with Darya (Nicole LaLiberte), a pretty redhead in hotpants and a pink silk jacket. "It's a world of truck drivers," Buella says drily.

Mr. C's next victim is Phyllis Hastings, who finds him in her house after visiting Bill in jail. Played by socialite Cornelia Guest, Phyllis had taunted Bill over his secret romance with Ruth, and her own affair with their lawyer George. "You follow human nature perfectly," Mr. C says – as if Phyllis, too, is not fully human – before shooting her with George's gun.

In a high-rise office block in neon-lit Las Vegas, a drumbeat sounds. Duncan Todd hands his fresh-faced assistant, Roger (Joe Adler) a payment, and asks him to "tell her she has the job." Played by Patrick Fischler (who also had a key role in Lynch's *Mulholland Drive*), Todd seems overcome with dread. "Why do you let him make you do

these things?" Roger asks. "Never have someone like him in your life," Todd responds. For the time being, 'he' and 'she' remain nameless.

The naming of Darya and Ray brings to mind Oscar Wilde's *The Picture of Dorian Gray*, with Darya the comely bait and Ray a wheedling con-man. "I have something you need," he goads Mr. C as they meet again in a diner. "I don't need anything, Ray," Mr. C snaps back. "I want." After Jack (Steve Baker) gives him a new car, Mr. C rubs the mechanic's cheeks together; a controlling gesture which mirrors a scene between Leland Palmer and his daughter, Laura, in *Fire Walk With Me*. Mr. C later tells Darya that Jack is dead, and then kills her for conspiring against him with "that fucker Ray." Her bloodied head resembles Ruth Davenport's as he smothers her with a pillow, and enlists another accomplice, the lusty Chantal, to 'clean up' his motel room. He plugs a black box into his laptop, using the device to contact Phillip Jeffries. But the long-lost FBI agent evades Mr. C's questions while hinting that he knows all about his nefarious plans.

Meanwhile in Twin Peaks, Chief Deputy Hawk follows up a call from Margaret Lanterman, the 'Log Lady', with a nocturnal trip into Ghostwood Forest. Armed with a flashlight, he makes his way to Glastonbury Grove, the enchanted ring of sycamore trees which first led Cooper to the red room. On his return to the Sheriff's Station, Hawk begins searching through old case files related to the murder of Laura Palmer, which brought Cooper to Twin Peaks. At her desk, receptionist Lucy quizzes an insurance salesman, wondering which Sheriff Truman he wants to see. She is also confused by cellular phone technology; after Frank Truman walks through the door mid-call, she falls off her chair in shock.

In Sarah Palmer's living room, little has changed. She sits watching television on the same afghan-covered couch, with her dead daughter's photo just visible on a nearby table. The long-time widow rises briefly to top up her drink, or toss another cigarette butt into an already overflowing ashtray. She watches grainy footage of animal brutality on repeat, also reflected in the mirror behind her. The second episode ends at the Roadhouse, where Ruth Radelet – looking for all the world like a 21st century Julee Cruise – sings 'Shadow,' a synth-driven ballad, with her band Chromatics.

In the red room, an older Laura Palmer appears to Cooper: "I am dead, yet I live." She raises her hand to her face, which unfolds to reveal a dazzling white light. Laura moves towards him, and smiling sweetly, whispers something in his ear. Then she backs off and flies upward, screaming. The One-Armed Man, Cooper's newfound spirit guide, leads him into another, identical room, where a mournful Leland Palmer asks him to "Find Laura." Cooper then meets the Evolution of The Arm, who tells him that his doppelganger "must come back in before you can go out." As Cooper peers through the red curtains that enclose this portal, he sees Mr. C driving, and the chevron floor quakes beneath him. He emerges from the glass box, floating like a man reborn in white noise, evoking the stark aesthetic of Lynch's debut film, *Eraserhead*.

The third and fourth episodes were also released consecutively. After leaving the glass box room, Cooper finds himself on the roof of a building, amid a vast, purple ocean. He goes back inside and enters another room. The interior is bathed in red light, and he sits beside Naido, a Japanese woman whose eyeless face resembles victims of the US atom bombs detonated in 1945. Their hands touch, and she traces his face until a loud banging noise distracts him. He walks over to a box engraved with the number '15' (also the number of remaining episodes.) After leaving together, they climb a ladder and pass through a trapdoor, landing on a black box. Naido pulls a lever and there is a surge of electricity as she falls into space. Looking down, Cooper sees the face of Major Briggs, who says "Blue Rose." (In *Fire Walk With Me*, we learned that 'blue rose' was a code-name for the unusual cases investigated by Cooper and his FBI colleagues.)

Back inside, the number on the box has changed to '3.' A woman known only as 'American Girl' is sitting by a fire. She was formerly Ronette Pulaski, Laura's friend who narrowly escaped being killed alongside her. Whether Ronette is still alive now is unclear, but it would appear her trauma has created a spirit double. "When you get there, you will already be there," she tells Cooper, who has another vision of Mr. C on the highway. The banging starts again, and American Girl warns him, "You'd better hurry up, my mother's coming." His face melts as he passes through the numbered box, leaving his shoes behind.

In the series' primary 'real-world' location of Las Vegas, as middle-aged businessman Dougie Jones – Kyle MacLachlan in a third guise – sits on a bed with a call-girl (Nafessa Williams.) After Dougie remarks that his arm feels 'tingly,' and fingers the jade owl-cave ring last seen in *Fire Walk With Me*. As his companion, also named Jade, leaves the bedroom to take a shower. After trying to get up, Dougie collapses, then crawls to the bathroom and back again. He stares at the open socket on the wall, and vomits on the carpet. At the same time, Mr. C loses control and his car crashes. After regaining consciousness, he also vomits. Highway patrolman arriving on the scene find cocaine – a gun and a dog's leg in the back of the car – take him to Yankton Prison.

Dougie finds himself in the red room. "Someone manufactured you for a purpose," the One-Armed Man tells him, "but now I think that's been

fulfilled." As he replies dully, "That's weird," the ring slips from Dougie's finger, and (rather like Sam and Tracey), his head goes up in smoke. Dougie disappears, leaving behind a gold seed. Cooper passes through the open socket, and after Jade hears an explosion, she finds him lying on the floor. Although thinner and more dapper than Dougie, she assumes it is him. She leads him out of the house, and noticing his dazed manner, drives him to the Silver Mustang Casino. Cooper is now living in Dougie's shoes, and seems to have regressed mentally. Passing from one slot to machine to another, he repeatedly hits the jackpot, parroting a gambler's cry: "Hello-oo-oo!" A bag lady (Linda Porter) approaches him, and he points her towards a machine where she, too, strikes it lucky. A casino supervisor (played by producer Sabrina Sutherland) surveys the chaotic scene.

At FBI headquarters in Philadelphia, Gordon Cole and Albert Rosenfeld are discussing the murders of Sam and Tracy with a junior agent, Tammy Preston. A portrait of Franz Kafka (who penned Lynch's favourite novella, *Metamorphosis*) hangs on the wall. Cole then takes a call in his office from a man who says he is Cooper. Having agreed to secure his release from Yankton, Cole tells Albert and Tammy to prepare for a trip to "the black hills of South Dakota." But first we retreat to the Roadhouse where the Cactus Blossoms perform 'Mississippi,' an Everly-esque ode to a girl waiting "somewhere on the shore," recalling the discovery of Laura Palmer's body in the original series.

Cole notifies his new Chief of Staff, ushered in by secretary Bill Kennedy (played by veteran TV star Richard Chamberlain.) David Duchovny reprises his role as the transgender FBI agent, Denise Bryson (one of the first non-binary characters seen on mainstream TV.) "When you became Denise," Cole says passionately, "I told all of your colleagues, those clown comics, to fix their hearts or die."

After collecting his winnings from a stressed-out manager, Cooper – or Dougie, as he is now identified – is driven away in a limousine. All he knows about his home is that it's on Lancelot Court (one of several street names that reference Arthurian legend) and has a red door. As the driver helps him out, Dougie hears an owl hooting. In the original series, the owls of Ghostwood Forest exuded menace. And perhaps even on this quiet suburban street, the Giant's message to Cooper may still hold true: "The owls are not what they seem."

Dougie is greeted by his wife, Janey-E, who slaps him on the face. He has missed Sonny Jim's birthday, she berates him, pausing for breath only when she discovers his large sack of cash. "This is the most wonderful, horrible day of my life!" she sighs. The next morning, Cooper sees his spirit guide – the One-Armed Man – who tells him, "You were tricked."

Sonny Jim – it would be hard to pick a more generic name – gives his father a thumbs-up, a gesture he gamely returns. Cooper then goes downstairs for breakfast in Dougie's lime-green jacket, tie hanging over his head. As Janey-E makes pancakes, Sonny Jim takes care of his dad. Played by ten-year-old Pierce Gagnon, he radiates innocent joy, yet is more self-aware than the adults around him. As Dave Brubeck's 'Take Five' plays over this family scene, Dougie nearly scalds himself with a sip of coffee.

As Hawk searches for clues at the Twin Peaks Sheriff's Station, another old face joins him in a new role – Bobby Briggs, teenage delinquent turned police officer. Bobby sees his former girlfriend's photograph laid out on the conference table, and bursts into tears to the strains of 'Laura's Theme.' Sheriff Frank Truman – who has replaced his ailing brother, Harry – is introduced to Wally Brando (Michael Cera), son of Chief Deputy Andy and his wife, Lucy.

In the original series, Lucy was unsure who the father of her child was but chose to marry Andy. Wally Brando's offbeat persona – an affectionate parody of Marlon Brando's biker role in The Wild One – suggests he may be the progeny of Lucy's dandyish ex-beau, Dick Tremayne. But Wally – perhaps named after Brando's best buddy, Mister Peepers star Wally Cox – loves his chosen family, as he tells a befuddled Frank in a comically surreal diatribe. "My dharma is the road," he declares, but his heart will remain in Twin Peaks.

After arriving at Yankton Prison, Cole speaks with Mr. C from behind a screen. As the man who would be Cooper says it is "YREV good to see you" and raises his thumb in reverse, Cole and his cohorts sense something is wrong. "I've been working undercover with Phillip Jeffries," Mr. C tells Cole, adding in his deep, robotic monotone, "I'm a little behind schedule." After bidding his 'old friend' goodbye, Cole urges Warden Murphy (James Morrison) not to release him.

Outside, the light is bathed in blue. Sending an irate Tammy to a nearby canteen, Cole and Albert watch the willowy, blue-suited agent whose undulating walk evokes the famous rear shot of Marilyn Monroe in Niagara, then billed as 'the longest walk in movie history.' While this is most likely coincidental, Lynch and Frost had first attempted a Monroe biopic, the shelved Goddess, before creating Twin Peaks. Marilyn's influence is particularly evident in the characterisation of Laura Palmer, and 'women in trouble' often feature in Lynch's work.

Albert confesses that some years ago, he authorised Cooper to give some information to Phillip Jeffries, via an FBI contact in Columbia. This is a case for the Blue Rose Task Force, they concur:

"Doesn't get any bluer." Back at the Roadhouse, all-female synth trio Au Revoir Simone perform an ethereal 'Lark,' in the first of two appearances.

Snake Eyes

Subsequent episodes were released one by one, and broadcast on Sunday nights. The fifth instalment begins in Las Vegas, where a dark-haired, nail-biting woman named Lorraine (Tammie Baird) is frantically calling two hitmen hired to kill Dougie Jones, as delegated by Duncan Todd. She then punches a series of numbers into a black box not unlike the one used by Mr. C. We then cut to an alleyway in Buenos Aires, where yet another black box lights up. (The Argentine city also featured briefly in Fire Walk With Me, where Phillip Jeffries was searching for someone named Judy.)

The hitmen drive by Rancho Rosa, a deserted housing development where Dougie had his assignation with Jade. Spotting his abandoned car, they plant a device underneath it. A little boy from a nearby house leaves his drugged-out mother (Hailey Gates) slumped over a table, crosses the road and peers under the car. A group of hoodlums scare him off and open the door to the car, which then explodes. As the boy hurries home, his mother awakes to a brief burst of 'Frank 2000', a track from Lynch and Badalamenti's 'dark jazz' album, Thought Gang. In a previous episode, the woman was seen downing pills with whiskey, and in a rare moment of clarity, she yelled "1-1-9!" – the emergency number in reverse. They are the last remaining residents of Rancho Rosa, bearing witness to the evils that occur there. Seen only by the audience and the ill-fated hoodlums, their role is similar to the Chalfonts, the trailer park residents who departed without trace after neighbour Teresa Banks was murdered in Fire Walk With Me.

In Buckhorn, Constance Talbot has completed an autopsy on the headless male body found in Ruth Davenport's bed. Inside his stomach is a wedding ring, engraved "From Janey-E to Dougie." Fingerprints have been traced to Major Garland Briggs. The information is delivered to the Pentagon in Arlington, Virginia; and clearly, it's not the first time Briggs has crossed their radar. "Sixteen hits in twenty-five years," Colonel Davis (Ernie Hudson) tells Lieutenant Cynthia Knox. The colonel's name may be a nod to Don Davis, who played Major Briggs in the original series. (The lieutenant is played by Adele René, who also narrated Mark Frost's audiobooks.)

From within his cell at Yankton Prison, Mr. C looks at the mirror and sees the demonic spirit, Killer Bob. "You're still with me," he says. "That's good." In the final scene of the original series, Cooper's double smashed his face into a mirror and Bob looked back. It seems their pact is still strong. Later, Warden Murphy permits Mr. C a

telephone call; but when he dials, a surge of electricity shakes the entire building. "The cow jumped over the moon," the prisoner says, and lays down the receiver. In Buenos Aires, the black box disintegrates in the alleyway.

Dougie looks in the mirror and by contrast, finds himself (or Cooper) looking back. When leaving for work, he glances at Sonny Jim and sheds a tear. This may be a dawning recognition from Cooper of the family life he has missed. Janey drives Dougie to the office of Lucky 7 Insurance, and a helpful colleague gives him coffee. He stands at the front of a crowded elevator, eyes fixed on the wall; and as his co-workers file out, he loiters between the automatic doors. McLachlan excels in playing these scenes of absurdist physical comedy, recalling one of Lynch's favourite movies, *Monsieur Hulot's Holiday* (starring Jacques Tati.) The reborn Cooper's difficulties in readjusting to life on the terrestrial plane give him the air of a stroke victim, and it may be a satirical commentary on the fast-moving corporate world that Dougie's fellow employees are only mildly concerned by his odd behaviour.

At a board meeting, Anthony Sinclair is talking to Lucky 7's boss, Bushnell Mullins, about an alleged case of arson when Dougie interrupts, saying flatly, "He's lying." A perplexed Mullins calls Dougie into his office, and hands him the case files. On the wall is a framed poster of 'Battling Bud Mullins' as a young boxer. He is played by veteran actor Don Murray, who made his screen debut opposite Marilyn Monroe in *Bus Stop* (1956.) Mullins also shares a first name with Bushnell Keeler, who initiated a teenage David Lynch into 'the art life.' Naming Dougie's boss after him is a tribute to their student-mentor relationship.

While the Jones family may be $425,000 richer, behind the scenes at the Silver Mustang – and under the watchful eye of billionaire Vegas recluse Howard Hughes, as pictured on the wall – the luckless manager is beaten by the casino's owners, Rodney and Bradley Mitchum (in homage to film noir anti-hero Robert Mitchum, who had worked for Hughes in Hollywood.) Three showgirls, identically clad in pink tutus, lean against the wall. Freely disassociating, the middle blonde waves her gloved arm in the air (evoking Laura's cryptic gestures to Cooper in the red room.)

In Twin Peaks, former high-school football hero Mike Nelson interviews Steven Burnett for a job. He dismisses Steven angrily, and we soon find out why. At the RR Diner, Steven's wife Becky delivers bakery goods and asks her mother, long-time waitress Shelly, for money. She then goes outside where Steven is sitting in a red, open-top car. In a sour replay of Shelly's past romances, the couple bicker until Becky gives Steven the money, and he shares a pinch of white powder. After taking a hit, her mood quickly becomes euphoric. Amanda Seyfried's long blonde hair and girlish features suggest another drug-enamoured beauty, the young Laura Palmer. Lynch frames

Becky's face in a doe-eyed close-up while her mind drifts away to the Paris Sisters' 1961 hit, 'I Love How You Love Me.'

At home on White Tail Peak, Lawrence Jacoby was earlier seen spray-painting shovels hanging down from a rail. Having removed his overalls, he dons the theatrical garb of online alter-ego Dr. Amp, to begin his latest broadcast: "It's seven o'clock. Do you know where your freedom is?" His psychiatric license long since revoked, the lifelong eccentric now resides in a humble trailer. Among his viewers are an appreciative Nadine Hurley, alone at her desk; and Jerry Horne, getting high in the forest. Ben's wayward brother seems to be taking his latest business venture – medical marijuana – a little too far. "The fucks are it again," Dr. Amp rages, urging his followers to "shovel your way out of the shit." This grand polemic then cuts to a commercial for Dr. Amp's Golden Shovels (Only $29.99.)

At the Roadhouse, Richard Horne is sitting alone, while Trouble – a band featuring Lynch's son, Riley, and diagetic composer Dean Hurley – perform 'Snake Eyes,' a guitar-led instrumental chased by ominous drums. A bartender asks Richard to stop smoking, but in true 'bad-boy' fashion, he just sneers. He then hands a cigarette pack stuffed with dollar bills to Deputy Sheriff Chad Broxtowe, who mentions having picked up a drunk on the road that night. A young girl in the next booth approaches Richard, and he pulls her towards him viciously. We're left wondering if he might be related to Audrey Horne, who has yet to make her entrance. In the original series, Audrey was infatuated with Dale Cooper. However, Richard's malevolent aura is more akin to Cooper's doppelganger.

As Dougie's working day comes to an end, he lingers outside by the brass statue of a cowboy pointing into the distance, tracing its boots to a lonesome Johnny Jewel instrumental, 'Windswept.' The sculpture was modelled on a snapshot of Lynch's father. As night falls, a security guard takes pity on Dougie and drives him home. While Janey-E thanks the guard, Dougie seems preoccupied with his badge. She sends him upstairs to say goodnight to Sonny Jim, and they play together, turning a nightlight on and off with handclaps. Janey-E angrily confronts Dougie about his infidelity with Jade, and sets him to work on Bushnell's case files. As Cooper, he has a vision of the One-Armed Man, who tells him, "You have to wake up. Don't die."

The next day, Dougie presents his work to Bushnell Mullins, who is baffled by his "childish scribbles": a ladder, a staircase, and a black spot next to Anthony Sinclair's name. After a few moments, however, Bushnell detects an underlying logic. "You're an interesting fellow," he says. Elsewhere in Las Vegas, Duncan Todd prints out a message from Mr. C: the sheet is blank, except for a black spot. And in a gruesome assault, diminutive assassin 'Ike the Spike' hacks Lorraine to death with an ice-pick, at the behest of Mr. C or other dark forces. Lorraine's inability to eliminate Dougie has been her undoing.

A furious, yet purposeful Janey-E meets two small-time criminals at high noon in a children's playground "on the corner of Guinevere and Merlin, by the mall." They are demanding repayment for a $52,000 gambling debt incurred by Dougie Jones. "We are the 99 Per-Centers," she scolds them crossly. "We are living in a dark, dark age, and people like you are part of the problem!" She hands them $25,000 – "my first, last, and only offer" – and stomps off. "Tough dame!" the smitten hood sighs.

In Twin Peaks, Richard Horne meets with Red, a gangster kingpin who claims to have magical powers, and is currently trafficking a Chinese designer drug, 'Sparkle,' from across the Canadian border. He speaks in ominous riddles, and mockingly calls Richard 'Kid.' Played by Balthazar Getty (who previously starred in *Lost Highway*), Red might be a latter-day incarnation of Pierre Tremond, the precocious boy who lived with his grandmother Alice and performed magic tricks. Although believed dead, they seemed to manifest at will. Otherwise known as the Chalfonts, the Tremonds were last seen at a gathering of Lodge inhabitants in the room above the Convenience Store (a Black Lodge portal) in *Fire Walk With Me*.

Carl Rodd, elderly caretaker of the Fat Trout Trailer Park, hitches a ride to the edge of town and sits on a park bench, gazing up at the trees. A young mother and son pass by, and he smiles. The camera follows them to a crossroads, where a truck driver stops to let the boy cross. A drug-crazed Richard Horne, enraged by his humiliating encounter with Red, runs over the child in a stolen truck before driving off, screaming: "I told you to get out of the way!" As the hysterical mother (Lisa Coronado) cradles her dead son, a crowd gathers and Carl comforts her, while gazing at a flame in the sky. This is the same vision that guided Dougie to his jackpots at the casino, and so it seems that Carl is also among the gifted. In *The Secret History of Twin Peaks*, Mark Frost reveals that many years ago, Carl was one of three children abducted in Ghostwood Forest (Margaret Lanterman was another.) None of them could remember what happened during their absence, and each returned with a triangular symbol etched onto their shoulder.

In the men's bathroom of the Sheriff's Station, Hawk bends down to retrieve a coin, and notices a brand name on the door: "Nez Perce," after an Indian tribe whose stolen land is referenced in *The Secret History of Twin Peaks*. Remembering Margaret's advice that the missing clue would have "something to do with your heritage,"

Hawk hacks the door apart, and finds inside the missing pages of Laura Palmer's diary, concealed years ago by Leland Palmer. His discovery is interrupted by Deputy Chad, who demands to know what he is doing. When Hawk brusquely tells him to use the ladies' room, Chad whines, "Why are you always against me?"

As Chad returns to his desk, he finds Doris Truman berating her husband, Frank, over a leak at home, and for not fixing her father's car. One of Twin Peaks' many frustrated wives, Doris is played by Candy Clark, formerly David Bowie's leading lady in *The Man Who Fell to Earth*. When dispatcher Maggie (Jodee Theleen) reminds Chad that the Trumans' son committed suicide after serving in the military, he mocks this family tragedy. At the Roadhouse, Sharon Van Etten echoes the savagery of recent events with the mournful 'Tarifa.'

The seventh episode finds ageing stoner Jerry Horne lost in the woods, his car stolen. He calls his brother Ben in a panic: "I think I'm high!"

In the Sheriff's Station, Hawk and Frank read the lost pages of Laura's diary. "Now I know it isn't Bob. I know who it is," she wrote, having realised her abuser's true identity. She then relates a message from a dream: "The good Dale is in the lodge and he can't get out." This dream was enacted in *Fire Walk With Me*, and the messenger was Annie Blackburn (Heather Graham), the woman whom Cooper loved and sacrificed his soul to save. The final episode of *Twin Peaks* had ended with Cooper's double taunting his mirror image with the words, "How's Annie?" Disappointingly, she is absent from the new series. But in *Twin Peaks: The Final Dossier*, Mark Frost writes that Annie is still living, albeit in a vegetative state. Once a year, at the same time and date, she answers: "I'm fine."

Frank uses Skype to contact Dr. Will Hayward, the last person to have seen Cooper alive. He recalls that Cooper was in hospital, but had discharged himself. Hayward saw him leaving the ICU, and assumed he was visiting Audrey Horne (who had been seriously injured in an explosion at the town's bank.) "He was acting mighty strange … with that strange face," Doc says. It was Cooper's doppelganger he saw that day, suggesting what some viewers suspected: that he captured Audrey at her most vulnerable and raped her.

Meanwhile, Deputy Andy is speaking with a long-haired, bearded man (Edward 'Ted' Dowling), outside what looks a lot like Dead Dog Farm, which Cooper had considered purchasing in the original series. The remote property has long been associated with criminal activity. The man, named only as a 'farmer,' is deeply spooked. His stolen truck has been found in a nearby field where Richard abandoned it. The farmer is too scared to answer Andy's questions, but agrees to meet him later on Sparkwood Road. He never arrives.

Lieutenant Cynthia Knox arrives in Buckhorn, and asks if Major Briggs' fingerprints are attached to a body. "There's a body alright," Dave Macklay says (giving us the episode's titular line.) Constance Talbot shows her the body of a man in his late forties, who died five or six days previously. Briggs, who disappeared twenty-five years ago, would now be seventy. Cynthia goes into the hall and calls Colonel Davis at the Pentagon. As she speaks, a large, shadowy figure passes by, and she shudders.

In Philadelphia, Gordon Cole and Albert Rosenfield visit the apartment of Diane Evans, former assistant to Agent Cooper. Fans of the original series will remember Cooper dictating his daily activities to Diane on a tape recorder. It was even speculated that Diane never existed, except in his imagination. A deleted scene from *Fire Walk With Me* (collected in *The Missing Pieces* as part of the 2014 Blu-Ray release) shows the young Cooper flirting with an unseen Diane while standing outside her door.

Played by Lynch's favourite actress and 'muse', Laura Dern, this Diane is a long way from the beloved Girl Friday of yore. She wears a platinum blonde wig and a red kimono, and smokes constantly. Her old colleagues are not welcome; at each request she snaps back, "Fuck you." Nonetheless, Cole finally persuades her to visit Cooper in Yankton Prison. While airborne, Tammy points out that the thumbprint on Cooper's prison I-D is the inverse of Dale Cooper's from years ago. On arrival, Diane confronts Cooper's double alone, from behind a screen. She asks him if he remembers the last time they met: "I'll always remember that night at your house," he replies. "I'll never forget it," she adds bitterly, while Cooper smirks: "I think you're upset with me, Diane."

"It's not the Dale Cooper I knew," she tells Cole outside. "It isn't time passing, it's something here," she sobs, hand on heart. She hugs Cole, and something in her touch alarms him. Then she raises up a mini-bottle of vodka. "Cheers to the FBI," she adds brokenly.

After they leave, Mr. C heads to Warden Murphy's office. "The dog leg – the other three legs went out with the information you're thinking about now," he says, teasing his jailer with the names of Joe McCluskey and the mysterious 'Mr. Strawberry.' His blackmail has the desired effect, and Mr. C demands Murphy release him along with Ray Monroe, who is also being held. That night, the warden looks on fearfully as the two men drive away.

At Lucky 7 Insurance, Dougie is questioned by three detectives about his missing car, now a burnt-out wreck on Rancho Rosa. His monosyllabic replies are interrupted by the arrival of Janey-E, who blames the detectives for not telling

him sooner. As Dougie and his wife leave the office, Ike the Spike races towards them, ice-pick in hand. In a brief reawakening, Cooper springs into action. The Arm appears, telling him to "squeeze his hand off." A maimed Ike flees the scene, and the action cuts to a TV news report.

In the Great Northern Hotel, Beverly Paige tells Ben about a peculiar hum emanating from the corner of Room 315, where Cooper stayed many years ago (and where he was shot by Josie Packard, herself later killed in the hotel.) Ben will later compare the sound to "the ringing of a monastery bell." An old-fashioned key to the same room has just arrived in the mail, sent from Las Vegas by Jade, who found it in her truck after it slipped out of Dougie's pocket. Ben explains that Cooper was an FBI agent, investigating the death of Laura Palmer. Who was she, Beverly wonders? "That is a long story," Ben replies.

There is chemistry between them, but Ben seems reluctant to take it further. In the past, he was a philanderer who even dallied with Laura, then at high school with his daughter Audrey. Now, it seems, he wants to be a better man. It's also possible that Beverly reminds him of Audrey, as they would now be around the same age. Although his relationship with Audrey was often conflicted, it seemed likely that she would eventually join him in running the family business. Could her absence be connected to Ben's change in attitude? As Beverly arrives home that night, a nurse is leaving. "It's been a rough day," she says. Inside the house, Beverly's invalid husband is sitting by the fire, and asks why she is so late. "I know you're suffering," she tells him, "but do not use that to fuck with me." It is the only glimpse we will get of Beverly's private life, and like other marriages in Twin Peaks, it is steeped in pain and heartache.

At an empty Roadhouse, a lackey sweeps the floor while Sam & Dave's 'Green Onions' plays. This goes on for several minutes, as Lynch tests his viewers' patience. If he is sweeping up the story's loose ends like sawdust, why are some left behind? Walter Olkewicz, who played sleazy Jacques Renault in the original series, takes a call from behind the bar. "The Roadhouse has been owned by the Renault family for fifty-seven years," he boasts, and as 'Jean-Michel' argues with a customer who complains that he was only sent one underage girl instead of the two he requested, it is revealed that the Roadhouse's other trade is still thriving.

Over at the RR Diner, business is brisk. Last seen playing guitar at the Roadhouse, Bing (Riley Lynch) rushes into ask if anyone's seen Billy, whose identity will soon become a matter of debate among fans. As another tune from the past (Santos and Johnny's 'Sleepwalk') plays on the jukebox, it is undercut by industrial noise. Twin Peaks has often seemed like a town lost in time, and now, as we watch customers appear and disappear, it seems that time itself has hit a warp.

She's Gone Away

The eighth episode begins in darkness, with Mr. C and Ray driving up to a wooded area after leaving Yankton Prison. As Ray gets out to "take a leak," Mr. C retrieves the gun left by Warden Murphy in the glove compartment. This scene recalls Cooper's camping trip in Ghostwood Forest with Major Briggs in the original series. While Cooper was 'taking a leak,' Briggs vanished into thin air. History is about to repeat itself as a call of nature triggers unexpected consequences. "Tricked you, fucker!" As Mr. C prepares to take aim, Ray turns around and shoots him. But as Cooper's double falls to the ground, a group of unkempt men advance from the woods to encircle him, laying their hands on his chest and rubbing blood on his face. A large bubble emanates from Mr. C's belly, with the leering face of Killer Bob ballooning. A terrified Ray makes a quick call to Phillip Jeffries, and drives off into the night.

Back at the Roadhouse, an MC (played by J.R. Starr) introduces Nine Inch Nails' 'She's Gone Away', seemingly another reference to the evil unleashed by the loss of Laura. And in the Dakota woods, Mr. C sits up.

The remainder of the episode is mostly filmed in black and white. We go back in time – July 16, 1945, at 5:29 a.m. – in the desert at White Sands, New Mexico, where a nuclear weapon (code name 'Trinity') was secretly detonated in a test explosion for the 'Manhattan Project.' In a breathtaking sequence, David Lynch recreates the mushroom cloud which rose up on that morning, to the sounds of Kyzysztof Penderecki's 1960 composition, *Threnody to the Victims of Hiroshima*. After reverting to the *Eraserhead*-inspired white noise background which has already appeared during Cooper's flight from the red room, the footage briefly bursts into colour and a plague of insects covers the earth.

Lynch then guides us towards the Convenience Store seen in *Fire Walk With Me*. From outside, it resembles the garage from Edward Hopper's 1940 painting, *Gas*. The woodsmen seen tending to Mr. C are now gathered at the store, when the Trinity explosion electrifies the building. They walk around the forecourt and back again, as if the same moment is happening over and over. We then see a stick man floating through space; the face of Bob. leering through the mushroom cloud; and the lost highways of America, in perpetual motion. Finally, we arrive at the subterranean plane glimpsed by Cooper after he smashed his way through the glass box. A giant rock fortress in the middle of the ocean sheds its skin, and we return to the tubular construction which Cooper and Naido navigated together. Like Cooper, we must pass through an open socket – one of the recurring images of this season's *Twin Peaks*, as the ceiling fan in Laura's house was in the original series – to step inside this mysterious construction. A voluptuous, dark-haired woman in a shimmering gown – billed as Senorita Dido – is sitting on a couch, listing to a nostalgic Badalamenti tune ('Slow 30s Room') on a phonograph. Her reverie is interrupted by incessant foghorn noise coming from another large tube in the same room. The spirit formerly known as 'The Giant' appears and flicks a switch, silencing the offensive sound. We follow him out of the room and up a grand staircase, leading into what resembles a 'dream palace' or old-time cinema. With a wave of his head, he turns on the screen and sees the frozen image of Bob's face in a mushroom cloud. The Giant levitates, and a spotlight glows around him. Senorita Dido enters the room, and we see her shadow. Bob's face vanishes, and rays of light stream from the Giant's head towards the screen, transforming into a golden orb as it reaches the cloud. The orb flies off the screen, and Dido catches it. She gazes in wonder as the smiling face of Laura Palmer fills the orb, and kisses it before letting it go. A globe appears on the screen, and the orb makes its way to Twin Peaks.

We then move forward in time, to August 5, 1956. In the New Mexico desert, an egg hatches and a large hybrid insect – the 'frogmoth' – crawls out. Nearby, a teen-age boy is walking a girl home. She finds a penny, and he says, "I hope it brings you good luck." Meanwhile, a woodsman lands in the desert. He is played by Robert Broski, whose regular job is as an Abraham Lincoln impersonator. The woods-man carries an unlit cigarette, and his skin is ashen (like the Log Lady's husband who died in a forest fire, and was seen above the convenience store in *Fire Walk With Me*; and the dark figure who lurks behind garbage cans in Lynch's 2001 film, *Mulholland Drive*.) He approaches a portly couple in a car, asking "Gotta light?" (This line gives the episode its title.) As he leans in, they become alarmed and drive away.

As the teenagers reach the girl's home, the boy asks for a kiss. After their innocent embrace, the girl walks into her house and sits on her bed, smiling dreamily. She turns on the radio, where the Platters' 'My Prayer' is playing. At the same time, the woodsman enters the radio station. A receptionist greets him in a perfect recreation of another Hopper painting, *Office at Night*. As the woodsman takes hold of her head, her uncertain smile is replaced by a final scream as she falls to the floor. The woodman enters the DJ booth and pulls the needle off the record. Grabbing the microphone, he repeats a sinister mantra:

"This is the water,
And this is the well.
Drink full,
And descend.
The horse is the white of the eye,
And dark within."

As the woodman's words fill the airwaves, we see more local residents – a waitress in a diner, a garage mechanic – flopping to the ground. The woodsman grasps the DJ's head, ensuring his grisly fate. He leaves the radio station, and the frogmoth climbs up to the open window of the girl's bedroom. Like the other residents she has fallen asleep, and in the final frame, the frogmoth crawls inside her gaping mouth. Some have speculated that the girl (played by Tikaeni Faircrest) might be a young Sarah Palmer; and in *The Final Dossier*, Mark Frost reveals she was raised in New Mexico. The frogmoth incident may explain why the adult Sarah was so unable to protect her daughter. 'Gotta Light?' stands apart from all other episodes, providing viewers with a creation myth linking the struggles of the show's characters to a wid-er psychic mutation in the post-nuclear age.

In the ninth episode we find a bloodied Mr. C walking down a tree-lined road the next morning. He is met at an isolated farmhouse by Hutch (Tim Roth), who works with his wife Chantal for Mr. C. As we see the unfortunate tenants "sleeping out back," it seems that this 'establishment' is South Dakota's answer to Dead Dog Farm. Roth plays Hutch as an amiable yes-man (and later, a ruthless hitman.) We last saw Jennifer Jason Leigh as Chantal in the motel scene of the second episode. She and Roth were previously paired in Quentin Tarantino's 2015 Western, *The Hateful Eight*, as members of an outlaw gang. Hutch clearly has no qualms about sharing his wife's affections with Mr. C, as he urges her to "give the boss-man a wet one." After cleaning up Mr. C – "I'll get the kit" – they furnish him with a new car, phone and gun. He uses the phone to send a cryptic text message: "Around the dinner table, the conversation is lively."

Meanwhile, Gordon Cole and his team are on a flight headed for Buckhorn, when he gets a call from Warden Murphy. "Cooper flew the coop?" Cole says incredu-lously.

In Las Vegas, Bushnell tells police that Dougie's recent problems are probably finan-cial – "in the insurance business, folks have been known to hold a grudge" – but, he concedes, "it's a damn strange business." Dougie was involved in a car crash about twelve years ago, he explains, and while he's usually a "slow and steady" worker, some "lingering effects" sporadically arise. As Bushnell leaves the detectives' office, he greets Dougie and Janey-E in the waiting room (which, incidentally, is a term also used to describe the red room.) Like the Trumans, the three officers are brothers named Fusco; but this inept trio seem to have more in common with the Three Stooges. A background check reveals little about Dougie, whose existence prior to 1997 is undocumented (although elsewhere in the Lynch universe, *Lost Highway* was released that year.)

In the waiting room, Dougie gazes at a U.S. flag while 'America the Beautiful' plays faintly; perhaps Cooper, still trapped inside Dougie, is reminded of his FBI days. He then gazes at the red stilettos worn by a passing secretary (an image associated with Audrey Horne.) One of the Fusco brothers has the bright idea of getting Dougie's red coffee mug tested for DNA. Then a lowly, but rather more competent desk sergeant (Jelani Quinn) informs them that local villain Ike the Spike is currently staying in a nearby motel. As he leaves his room, Ike is arrested.

At the Sheriff's Station in Twin Peaks, Lucy and Andy quarrel about an armchair they're planning to buy online (Lucy wants beige, Andy prefers red.) After Andy gives in, Lucy orders the red. In the home of Ben Horne's estranged wife Sylvia, their mentally impaired son Johnny runs amok, crashing into a bedroom wall against a framed photo of Snoqualmie Falls. As a young man, he had been taken under Laura's wing. Like Johnny, she had a framed picture on her bedroom wall; and although her picture was of another wall, both images denote entrapment. Laura's painting was given to her by the Tremonds, foreshadowing her death.

Bobby, Frank and Hawk visit the widowed Betty Briggs at home, and knows immediately why they have come. She leads them to Major Briggs' red armchair, and opens up the frame to retrieve a small stick-like device. "This is the chair," she says, beaming, as a new Angelo Badalamenti composition plays, flooding the room with love. ('This is the Chair' also gives this episode its title.)

After coffee with Betty, they return to the Sheriff's Station and eject a disgruntled Chad from the conference room. When Frank is unable to unlock the device, Bobby suggests they go outside. Frank and Hawk look on as Bobby throws the stick across the lawn, and chases it with boyish delight. The stick cracks open, and they find a tiny sheet of paper rolled up inside. The paper includes hand-drawn directions to an area of Ghostwood Forest often visited by Bobby and his father, which they named 'Jackrabbit's Palace.' They are directed to visit the area at 2:53 pm in two days' time. The paper also contains a transmission feed intercepted by Major Briggs in the original series. Cooper's name appears twice, reminding Hawk of Laura's diary entry about 'the Good Cooper.' He then realises there may be another Cooper, and perhaps it wasn't the 'Good Cooper' who emerged from Glastonbury Grove years before.

Back in the woods, Jerry Horne's "solitary sojourn of a creative nature" has gone off the rails. His car has been stolen (perhaps by Richard), and as his left foot takes on a life of its own, a hissing voice (not unlike the Evolution of The Arm) tells him, "I am not your foot." Jerry tries to shake it off, and loses his balance. His drug-induced folly sets the stage for a bucolic parody of Cooper's own journey.

In Buckhorn, Dave Macklay leads Cole, Albert and Tammy towards the headless man's body while Diane stays in the waiting room. When Macklay says she's not allowed to smoke, she protests: "It's a fucking morgue!" With her leopard-skin jacket and black tailored shirt, wide green slacks and red flat-heeled shoes, Diane harks back to the wise-cracking heroines of 1930s Hollywood: Marlene Dietrich, Katherine Hepburn, and Barbara Stanwyck. After the others leave, she checks her phone. Mr. C's message was clearly intended for Cooper's former secretary, and it rattles her nerves.

After Macklay brings the team up to date, Albert quips: "What happens in Season 2?" As they view the body, an unlikely flirtation is sparked between Albert and Constance, Buckhorn's deadpan pathologist. The hard-of-hearing Cole calls Albert away, and then in his usual manner, confers with him loudly enough for all to hear. Outside, they find Diane smoking. As she offers Cole a puff on her cigarette, Tammy looks on disapprovingly. "We used to smoke together way back when," Diane reminisces. "You remember?" Cole smiles wistfully, and a tense standoff ensues. The

contrasting body language of these two women reminds us that Tammy has supplanted Diane as the lone female in Cole's group.

Chrysta Bell is an accomplished singer-songwriter and model who has recorded two albums with David Lynch, and their partnership parallels that of Cole and Tammy. *Twin Peaks* was her first major acting role, and she proves her worth in the following scene where she gently, yet deftly questions Bill Hastings. In a metatextual touch, it is revealed that Bill kept a blog with Ruth Davenport, documenting their mutual interest in the paranormal. Presented in the gaudy, cluttered style of retro web design, The Search for the Zone can be accessed online.

Hastings is played by Matthew Lillard, best-known for his role as Shaggy in the live-action Scooby Doo movie. As he becomes increasingly distressed, his voice rises, and Lillard uses his comedic skills to bring pathos to Bill's confession. After telling Tammy that he and Ruth met Major Briggs in another dimension, he again denies any involvement in her murder but admits to dreaming about it. There are shades of Leland Palmer here, who was possessed by Bob when he killed his daughter. Bill's grief for his lost love is both touching and absurd, as he laments, "We were going to go scuba-diving!"

At the Roadhouse, DJ and producer Hudson Mohawke performs a synth instrumental, 'Human,' while two women chat in a booth. Bleached blonde, acne-scarred Ella (played by singer Sky Ferreira) has been fired from her waitressing job, but found work in another burger joint across the street. As her dark-eyed friend asks leading questions, Ella repeatedly scratches her armpit, which is covered in "some kind of wicked rash." This is the first in a series of parallel dramas enacted at the Roadhouse. Au Revoir Simone return with 'A Violent Yet Flammable World,' an apt description for the town of Twin Peaks.

TARA HANKS WAS BORN AND RAISED IN LONDON. SINCE THEN SHE HAS LIVED IN LANCASTER, DERBY AND NOW BRIGHTON. SHE IS MARRIED AND HAS TWO SONS.

WICKED BABY, TARA'S NOVELLA BASED ON THE EVENTS OF THE PROFUMO AFFAIR, WAS PUBLISHED IN 2004. AN EXTRACT HAS BEEN SHOWCASED ON THE OFFICIAL WEBSITE OF WHITBREAD-NOMINATED AUTHOR LAURA HIRD.

THE MMM GIRL, TARA'S NOVEL ABOUT THE LIFE OF MARILYN MONROE, IS WINNER OF THE UKA PRESS OPENING PAGES COMPETITION, AND WAS PUBLISHED IN 2007. EXTRACTS FROM THE MMM GIRL ARE FEATURED IN VOICES FROM THE WEB ANTHOLOGY 2006 AND FAN PHENOMENA: MARILYN MONROE (2015.)

CO-AUTHORED WITH ERIC WOODARD, JEANNE EAGELS: A LIFE REVEALED – THE FIRST FULL-SCALE BIOGRAPHY OF THE LEGENDARY ACTRESS IN MORE THAN EIGHTY YEARS – WAS PUBLISHED IN 2015.

TARA ALSO WRITES ABOUT ASPECTS OF POPULAR CULTURE FOR A VARIETY OF WEBSITES AND PUBLICATIONS (INCLUDING FOR BOOKS' SAKE, IMMORTAL MARILYN AND ART DECADES) AND MAINTAINS THE ES UPDATES BLOG. SHE IS CURRENTLY WORKING ON HER THIRD NOVEL.

FROM TARAHANKS.COM

For Every Part Of Me

six poems
by
Emily Clare Bryant

A Poem for my Father, Water and Stone

A year after you passed,
With wet steps and damp shoes
I rested my head against the porch's post
As if it were shoulder,
And swore I heard your voice
In the pitter patter of the rain
Tiny drops slid off the roof to railing
Above me a plane exceeded the sky,
With a soft smile, and a pinch of the heart
I pretended you were coming home

Eight months after you passed,
I caught your eyes in my reflection
For two days I brushed my teeth in the kitchen
In every photo of you in the house I heard
Your belly laugh, weekend pool, Bud-light belly,
Oregano, thyme, chopped onion belly
Redbox Friday, Fleetwood Mac loving belly
A belly that made the whole room feel
Full

Five months after you passed,
Mom introduced me to her new boyfriend
His white hair, the kind of white hair I never would see
On you, the kind of white hair that stung
Like Kentucky Snow air, the kind that stung
My cheeks like honey bees in June
When they are ready to die

Two months after you passed,
That flowered, brass chair on the deck
I sat and replayed your last three days,
As if they were my only memories
Your feathered organs and paperback skin,
There was nothing sadder than that salute
To ceaseless summer
It was like saying goodbye all over again

The day you passed I remember that
I held my breath and counted each line
On my hands, watched them heave themselves
Across my palms, they crossed paths

Like ravine became cobblestone, crossed paths
Like passenger window mountains became sketches
Of trees, they reached, and reached
And the sky wept for two worlds to collide again

My fingers became mountains that longed-for clouds,
My palms, a ravine, and I tossed stones in them
I hoped they could take me back to childhood
Reached, and reached, I'll reach
And eventually, we too,
Shall cross paths again

On Understanding my Mother, a Poem on Forgiveness

My mother has loud fingers
The kind that push you when still
She has words that move like a lifetime,
So fast you can almost miss them
She is withered lips, ready to spread when needed
She has a heart, I know it, it just sometimes hides
When needed
She's been hurt, and who hasn't?

My grandfather watched my mother grow
Into a woman six states away
I think about that on days when she forgets
To pick up the phone, my mother
All Italian, a potluck of a woman
She will bring to the table whatever is asked of her
She is the pasta, the risotto, the lasagna
She has yet to learn how to cook

My mother, with tawny eyes,
Eyes that don't need the sun to shine
Eyes that squint in dim light,
As if they've seen storms each time they've opened
My mother, historic introspective woman
She listens to me speak as if she is six states
Away, forever beautiful
Her mirror compresses her into a woman
She will forever recognize

My Nona died when I was six

Her arms were like heated blankets,
They wrapped me up when the world fell
Cold, and they wrapped my mother up as a child
On nights when her anger was thunder,
Her words, always a lifetime
My grandmother bolder, my mother dust
Ready to blow when the attic needed her to move
Suppressed on days when she'd lost her voice
To poverty

My mother, with vacant stare
And jokes that make the deck crumble
Below her, heart wrenched wine
In a plastic cup, A lonely woman,
She tells her stories
As if they just happened, they echo behind her
Yet she retells them with hope that their endings
Can change, my mother,
Who cannot always pick up the phone,
But needs someone to listen
I've learned

My father always said
To accept people's flaws and to love them
Regardless. I love her regardless,
I just wish she would hear me

Comparing Adolescent Depression to Adulthood

I lick rain off my cheeks
Make my cheeks like soft hills
Untouched, Unscathed
I paint the salt from these tears onto walls
Translate my feelings with a throat so dry
I can only write about

In the bath, water pollutes my mouth,
The garbage of words leftover meshes
With the smell of Lavender
Home grown, nostrils flared,
I've smelled this before

I covet homes, apartments

I live in for only a year, I bounce around
Like my thoughts dance among crowds,
And I love as if I've already lost

I sometimes get furrowed Brezhnev-brows,
Three wrinkles on the forehead when upset,
Like a note folded over, crinkled,
I pass myself off for someone else to read
There's adolescence in that
Adolescence in hating the past,
And on days I miss home,
When I really miss home,
I think of the parts of my adolescence
That weren't all that bad

Bare

My gum is smoke, nicotine in a chew My body, muse with a flare in flimsy lamp

Jeff looks at me, voice bitter vodka
And asks "Do you ever think you outlived yourself?"
My hands stained grey like water in an ashtray
Voice rough I reply
"I think we all have"

The paint on the walls are lucid to our words
Our thoughts are like clouds, mouths revel
The brim beauty of picturing a cup overflown
The windows tighten, shutter softly
For the air that kisses our bare elbows

I wonder how long I'll feel fifteen
Pink bottomed feet, still ready to run if asked
Whites of my eyes colored lamb fur
When widened, eyes that see small things
Like olive drab pillows on sofas,
Eyes that count the seconds
In between conversations

I feel fifteen still
And I hate the way it spills from my mouth
Fifteen like a curfew, I drown in my twenties
Where I need to go somewhere,

With nowhere to be
It's toilet water, fifteen
Like giving an answer when nobody asked
And its poison to feel that way
In my twenties

Where I go

There's a place I go when nobody's looking
Where my blood boils high on thick ice
And my eyelashes are half-frozen grass
Kissed by a sun on the days
It isn't sure it wants to be seen

There's a place I've found
Where my dreams crowd basement coolers,
They sit around, too patient for me
So I pretend to remember
And time burns blue,
Like late Tuesday television
Where I know I should be sleeping

There are days my body quits me
Cold turkey, days that rip seams out of pockets
To make the things I need disappear
I've got these days, these days
Where I'm past, with gapped teeth
Loose lips, unforgiving to the world
And floppy bangs hiding behind each ear

There are moments I want to trade my brain
For July air that sticks to North Limestone side-
walks,
A pair of faded black jeans in top drawer,
A first kiss,
Or pretty much anything that still knows
To forgive

But still I know of this place
Where my dad is still breathing
Where nights are still young to fresh face
And every walk I walk

Is like a night in December
Where I know something is coming
I just don't know what,
I just don't know what

After Speaking

When these words leave my lips
My mouth lingers, waiting, falling
I admire the ovals in empty air
With deadweight arms that hang beside me
Hoping to drag me away
From these limp words, heard,
Yet unsure of how my mouth even moves
When it's not asked to tango
With insecurities, or become wicked
To those who don't deserve to meet
Them

In pauses I'm afraid of my mouth
Planting seeds in other's brains
My meaning fried into the roots,
Each word jumps
Across my taste buds, runs around,
Makes themselves at home
Until I swallow them whole

Sometimes my mouth is like still water
Overly forgiving to each wave that passes
Words stick like salt on soggy leg,
Or feel like a sunburn in a cold shower
Enough to make me shiver in the heat

A dampen of my throat, a tickle in my belly
These words that sink through my toes
There are times when my tongue
Forces me to float

EMILY CLARE BRYANT
IS A KENTUCKY BASED
WRITER. HER FAVORITE
POETS ARE BYRON, POE,
DICKINSON AND BLAKE.
SHE AS WANTED TO BE A
WRITER SINCE THE THIRD
GRADE AND HER OTHER
INTERESTS INCLUDE
PSYCHOLOGY AND
SOCIOLOGY.

FOLLOW HER AT
INSTAGRAM AT
SADLUNAGIRL.

Front page photo from *The Ice Storm*.
Winter Photos by Jeremy R. Richey.
Street Scene Unknown.

"I've always admired the tradition of storytellers who sat in the public market and told their stories to gathered crowds. They'd start with a single premise and talk for hours - the notion of one story, ever-changing but never-ending."

~ Nicolas Roeg, 1928-2018~

AWAY
ZONE

Marquee Memories
Part 1
By
Jeremy R. Richey

That Summer of '76 had been the loneliest you had ever known. The months dragged along, and the days just got hotter and hotter, as you drifted from one theater to another searching...searching for the ghost of the girl who had overdosed in your bed earlier in the spring. Not able to find her, you mostly found yourself alone in scuzzy adult theaters during the day, because you got some odd comfort from being surrounded by all those other lonely men.

You occasionally made it into the night, and the first time you saw him was when he drove you to a double bill of *The Texas Chainsaw Massacre* and *Return of the Dragon*. You knew his name was Travis cause you could see it on his taxi license in front of you, but you two barely exchanged a word as he drove you to the theater. You recognized him though as he was one of those other lonely men who haunted those films during the day. You almost mentioned the coincidence to him but, before you could, you were already on the street watching his cab drive away.

You saw him throughout the summer, as the days grew longer and even more painful. You had taken to popping as many pain pills as you could afford to buy on the street, and one night in a daze you almost stepped out in front of his taxi after seeing a Swedish import called *Anita*. Gone to the point of being out, you made your way hazily into the heat drenched night.
By the mid-part of the summer you had mostly stopped going to the adult shows, as the faces of the men who sat close seemed to look more and more like yours. Not so surprisingly it was across the street from one of those porno houses where you saw Travis again, going in and quickly coming out with the most beautiful woman you had ever seen. You could see they were fighting as you made your way across the street towards them, away from the double shot of *Bucktown* and *The Eiger Sanction* you had just seen. As the beautiful blonde rushed away in a cab, Travis briefly glanced at you, with some recognition, but before you could say anything he was gone again into the sweat-soaked streets of the New York night.

You didn't see Travis again for a couple of months but you had read about him. Ironically his murderous meltdown helped set you back on a better track. You were surprised to see him one last time when he picked you up again to take you to another downtown movie. The back of the cab smelled like sweet perfume and, at one point, you thought he grinned at you in his rearview mirror, but you decided that it was just your new found sobriety playing a trick.

You elected to skip a last stand at the porn house you both used to visit, and instead you had him stop at a place showing Rudy Ray Moore's *Dolemite*. In need of a good laugh you felt like it was the perfect choice for the evening, which of course it was. Hopping out of the cab to pay, you were shocked when Travis reset the meter and said, "It's on me brother, it's on me." Not having even a moment to thank him, you watched his cab drive down the street into the deepest part of city. You stood and watched it until it was just two small red dots in the distance melting into yellow. You nodded silently to yourself, as you realized you would never see him again.

A version of this originally appeared at Moon in the Gutter

You have been reading the first volume of *Soledad*, an independent arts journal from Nostalgia Kinky Publications.
This issue was created in the fall of 2018, for the winter of 1979, in Frankfort, Kentucky.

Elvis Costello once said that his songs were about "Revenge and Guilt", in that order. That thought may, or may not, have anything to do with the what you are holding in your hands but it seemed worth sharing either way.

I compiled this mostly in the closing months of the second most tumultuous year of my life and I am greatly indebted to all of the talented artists that appear in this issue. Their great work and patience with me is eternally appreciated. Thanks also to Johnny Jewel and all of the extraordinary band at his Italians Do It Better label for helping to calm the anxiety filled days and sleepless nights that have been a constant companion to me this year.

Finally, I'd very much like to extend my heartfelt thanks to the following people for their compassion and kind words of encouragement throughout this past very difficult year:

Bill Ackerman, LaShane Arnett, Courtney Beckett, Daniel Bird, Dave Bookout, Jen Bookout, Justin Coffee, Brandon Colvin, Chris Cooley, Andrew Crawley, Samm Deighan, Ryan Dickins, Dave Ess, Dave Felter, Mollie Ficht, Bob Frye, Tiffany Gibbs, Michael Gonzales, Trace Hyatt, Kier-La Janisse, Jennifer Johnson-Armstrong, Salem Kapsaski, Kimberly Kane, Darin Kerr, Kelly Kerr, Susan Kerr, Sean Kinder, Steve Langton, Kimberly Lindbergs, Tim Lucas, Maria McKee, Jim Marshall, Aaron Elliot Olson, Liz Okeson, Francoise Pascal, Rachel Pickett, Candice Rankin, Amanda Reyes, Amy Martin, Melissa Martin, Jill Nelson, Janice Richey, Nancy Richey, Jeanne Silver, Casey Southworth, April Spicer, Bill Teck, Ashley West and William Wilson,

I'm very grateful to all of you and this issue wouldn't have been possible without your friendship and kindness...Jeremy

"Don't you get embarrassed when you think
about the way you were?
Yesterday the day before when you were
young with much to learn.
Aren't you glad it's your last term?
No more acting lowly worm.

Don't you feel ashamed at all the
bitterness you keep inside?
Does your ego save your face "I had a
go – I really tried"?
Now you know your leaders lied,
Does it stop you acting snide?
Or are you still a boy that cried
Tears now surely long since dried?"